International Series on Computer Entertainment and Media Technology

Series Editor

Newton Lee

The International Series on Computer Entertainment and Media Technology presents forward-looking ideas, cutting-edge research, and in-depth case studies across a wide spectrum of entertainment and media technology. The series covers a range of content from professional to academic.Entertainment Technology includes computer games, electronic toys, scenery fabrication, theatrical property, costume, lighting, sound, video, music, show control, animation, animatronics, interactive environments, computer simulation, visual effects, augmented reality, and virtual reality. Media Technology includes art media, print media, digital media, electronic media, big data, asset management, signal processing, data recording, data storage, data transmission, media psychology, wearable devices, robotics, and physical computing.

More information about this series at http://www.springer.com/series/13820

Barbaros Bostan

Editor

Gamer Psychology
and Behavior

 Springer

Editor
Barbaros Bostan
Department of Information Systems & Technologies
Yeditepe University
Istanbul, Turkey

ISSN 2364-947X   ISSN 2364-9488   (electronic)
International Series on Computer Entertainment and Media Technology
ISBN 978-3-319-29903-7   ISBN 978-3-319-29904-4   (eBook)
DOI 10.1007/978-3-319-29904-4

Library of Congress Control Number: 2016938528

This Springer imprint is published by Springer Nature
The registered company is Springer International Publishing AG Switzerland

Contents

About the Editor

 **Barbaros Bostan** is an Associate Professor in the Information Systems Department at Yeditepe University/Turkey. He has a Ph.D. in Information Systems (2007) from Marmara University, an M.B.A. (2003) from Yeditepe University, and a B.S. in Electronics and Communication Engineering (2001) from Istanbul Technical University. He worked as a post-doc researcher at **IDM Institute, Games Lab of the National University of Singapore,** between 2008 and 2010. His research areas include computer games, presence, interactivity, gamer psychology, gaming motivations, and player profiling. Bostan has teaching experience in the areas of computer games, computer networks, and interactive narrative. He is a member of the ACM, Computers in Entertainment Editorial Board. He reviews journal articles and book chapters for various journals and publishers, local and international (*Journal of Computer-Mediated Communication, Versita Open Access Books*, etc.).

About the Contributors

Sercan Altun has a B.S. in Industrial Engineering from Bilkent University. He is a game developer experienced in a wide variety of gaming projects. He started his career at a virtual world start-up as a game programmer. Later he cofounded a digital agency where he developed a variety of advergames, kinect-powered event games, social games, and mobile apps. He is currently studying M.A. in Game Design at Bahçeşehir University.

Mustafa Balkaya graduated from Istanbul University, Cerrahpasa Medical School. During his education, he worked as an editor at the Turkish version of the world-renowned gaming magazine "PC Gamer." He later moved to Berlin where he got his master's and Ph.D. degree on medical neurosciences in **Charite Medical School**. For postdoctoral studies, he spent two and a half years in **Harvard Medical School**, Massachusetts General Hospital. His research interests include stroke and poststroke emotional disturbances, depression, anxiety, and stress.

Güven Çatak started to write in video games magazines and also made short films while studying architecture at Istanbul Technical University. His shorts won several awards and were screened at various festivals. Now he is an Assistant Professor of Game Design at Bahçeşehir University, Communication Design Department. He is giving classes on motion and game design. He is also the founder director of Bahçeşehir University Game Lab (BUG) and Game Design Master

Program. His research areas are mainly gamification, game-based learning, and game art and design. He has a master's thesis on the usage of architecture in games and a Ph.D. thesis on using games in design education.

Metehan Irak is an Associate Professor of Psychology at Bahcesehir University, Turkey. He is also the director of Brain and Cognition Research Lab. He has a Ph.D. in Experimental Psychology from Hacettepe University, Turkey. He finished postdoctoral training at **University of Ottawa Institute of Mental Health Research, Canada,** and also worked as a part-time professor at the **University of Ottawa, School of Psychology**. His projects were funded by University of Ottawa Medical Research Fund, Ontario Center of Excellence for Child and Youth Mental Health, The Scientific and Technological Research Council of Turkey, and Bahcesehir University. He has been editor in chief of Turkish Psychological Articles since 2014.

Selcen Öztürkcan is an Associate Professor of Marketing and Program Coordinator of the MA and HR Management at Istanbul Bilgi University. She earned a B.Sc. in Engineering (1999) and an M.B.A. (2001). She continued her Ph.D. studies first at the **College of Business Administration of the University of South Florida** (2002–2003) and then at the Faculty of Management of the Istanbul Technical University (2003–2007). Her academic work mostly focuses on consumer behavior, online behavior, communication, and interactions. Her work could be followed from her website; www.selcenozturkcan.com

Gökhan Şahin received his undergraduate and master's degree from the Physics Department of Boğaziçi University and started his Ph.D. at the **Stevens Institute of Technology** and received his Doctorate degree at Boğaziçi University. He worked at Boğaziçi University, Stevens Institute of Technology, and Işık University. Presently, he is an Assistant Professor of Information Systems at Yeditepe University. He has several articles published in international journals covered by the SCI and SSCI.

Sercan Sengün is a Ph.D. candidate in Communication Sciences at Istanbul Bilgi University. His academic work mostly focuses on video game studies, interactive narrative, and gamification. He is also a game designer and a board member of Turkish Game Developers Association (Oyunder).

Tonguç Ibrahim Sezen is an Assistant Professor at Istanbul Bilgi University, Faculty of Communication. He holds a Ph.D. in Communications from Istanbul University, School of Social Sciences. During his doctoral studies, he visited **Georgia Institute of Technology**, School of Literature, Media, and Communication as a Fulbright scholar. His research interests include cross-media narration, game design, interactive storytelling, and toy studies. He is a member of the Games & Narrative research group.

Digdem Sezen is an Assistant Professor at Istanbul University, Faculty of Communications, and holds a Ph.D. from that same institution. During her Ph.D., she got the Fulbright scholarship for her doctoral studies and did research in the field of interactive storytelling, digital games, and experimental TV at **Georgia Institute of Technology**, School of Digital Media. She has presented and published papers and book chapters in many fields across this spectrum. She organizes conferences and events and gives workshops in these fields.

Özhan Tıngöy is a full Professor of Information Systems at Marmara University in Turkey. He has a Ph.D. in Marketing (1994), a M.A. in Industrial Relations (1992), and a B.A. at Economics (1987). He was the Vice Dean of Faculty of Communications between 2008 and 2009 and the Head of Department at Informatics between 2009 and 2012. He worked as a visiting Professor at the Computer and Information Sciences department of the **University of Strathclyde** between 2013 and 2014. His research areas include communication theory, mass communication theory, informatics ethics, informatics theory, knowledge management, and management information systems.

 **Ahmet Uysal** received his Ph.D. in Social Psychology from the **University of Houston** in 2010. He is a faculty member at Middle East Technical University, Department of Psychology in Ankara, Turkey. He is also a member of Game Technologies graduate program at METU and teaches a Psychology in Game Design course. His research interests include self-determination theory, self, well-being, and psychology in game design.

List of Contributors

Sercan Altun, B.S. Department of Game Design, Bahçeşehir University, Istanbul, Turkey

Mustafa Balkaya, Ph.D. Department of Physiology, Bahcesehir University, Istanbul, Turkey

Barbaros Bostan, Ph.D. Department of Information Systems and Technologies, Yeditepe University, Istanbul, Turkey

Dicle Çapan, M.A. Department of Psychology, Brain & Cognition Research Laboratory, Bahcesehir University, Istanbul, Turkey

Guven Catak, Ph.D. Department of Communication Design, Bahcesehir University, Istanbul, Turkey

Metehan Irak, Ph.D. Department of Psychology, Brain & Cognition Research Laboratory, Bahcesehir University, Istanbul, Turkey

Selcen Ozturkcan, Ph.D. Associate Professor, Istanbul Bilgi University, Istanbul, Turkey

Gokhan Sahin, Ph.D. Department of Information Systems and Technologies, Yeditepe University, Istanbul, Turkey

Sercan Sengun, M.A. Istanbul Bilgi University, Istanbul, Turkey

Tonguc Ibrahim Sezen, Ph.D. Department of Digital Game Design, Istanbul Bilgi University, Istanbul, Turkey

Digdem Sezen, Ph.D. Department of Radio, Television and Film, Istanbul University, Istanbul, Turkey

Can Soylu, M.Sc. Department of Psychology, Brain & Cognition Research Laboratory, Bahcesehir University, Istanbul, Turkey

Ozhan Tingoy, Ph.D. Department of Information Systems, Marmara University, Istanbul, Turkey

Ahmet Uysal, Ph.D. Department of Psychology, Middle East Technical University, Ankara, Turkey

Irem Gokce Yildirim, M.S. Game Technologies Program, Informatics Institute, Middle East Technical University, Ankara, Turkey

Part I
Neuro-psychology and Gaming

Part I
Neuropsychology and Learning

Chapter 1
Violent Video Games and Cognitive Processes: A Neuropsychological Approach

Metehan Irak, Can Soylu, and Dicle Çapan

Abstract The effects of violent video games on cognitive processes are still not clear. The main goal of this study was to investigate the effect of violent video games on different cognitive processes. A neuropsychological battery which consists of response inhibition, emotional memory, working memory, object recognition, and visual-spatial perception task was used to measure cognitive functions. Ninety eight participants were separated into three groups (namely addicted, risk group, and controls) based on the amount of time they spent for violent game playing (per week). DSM-based pathological game addiction symptoms and their scores are measured on game addiction scale. We found significant effects of excessive video game playing on working memory, object recognition, and response inhibition, whereas no significant differences were found among the groups on emotional memory and visual spatial perception.

Keywords Violent video game • Memory • Response inhibition • Neuropsychology

1.1 Introduction

Playing video games either through computers, game consoles (e.g., Nintendo Wii, Sony PlayStation), or handheld devices (cellular phones, tablets) are among the most popular leisure activities not just for adolescents but also for adults (Kirsch et al. 2005). Research has suggested that in American households, 93 % of children ages 8–18 have access to computer (Boot et al. 2008) and those children are playing video games 7–13 h/week (Bailey et al. 2010; Gentile and Anderson 2003). In one of the earliest studies Lynch (1983) stated that cognitive abilities (e.g., attention,

M. Irak, Ph.D. (✉) • C. Soylu, M.Sc. • D. Çapan, M.A.
Department of Psychology, Brain & Cognition Research Laboratory,
Bahcesehir University, Istanbul, Turkey
e-mail: metehan.irak@eas.bahcesehir.edu.tr; can.soylu@eas.bahcesehir.edu.tr;
dicle.capan@eas.bahcesehir.edu.tr

© Springer International Publishing Switzerland 2016
B. Bostan (ed.), *Gamer Psychology and Behavior*, International Series
on Computer Entertainment and Media Technology,
DOI 10.1007/978-3-319-29904-4_1

concentration, reaction time, visual tracking, memory, hand-eye coordination, mathematical ability, and verbal ability) are the determinants of playing video games; therefore, such cognitive processes could be affected by playing video games either positively or negatively. Ever since 1980s, a growing number of studies that investigate individual, cognitive, neurobiological, and societal outcomes of playing video games are observed.

The term addiction is misused frequently to refer to substances such as alcohol or drugs. However, the concept is much broader and it spreads to other constructs such as Internet, sex, gambling, television, or game. Over the past decades, Internet addiction (in a broad spectrum from gaming, shopping, and gambling to social networking) has been studied within the context of addictive behavior (Block 2008). Clinical investigations have shown that Internet addicts, like substance addicts, also experience a variety of bio-psychosocial symptoms including salience, mood modification, tolerance, withdrawal, conflict, and relapse (Sussman and Sussman 2011). With the growing Internet and game industries over the past decades, there have been increasing numbers of people considered as addicted to Internet and video games.

In addition to increasing arousal and aggressive thoughts, feelings, and behaviors, many studies have shown that obsessive-like behaviors (e.g., gambling addiction) also cause changes in brain activity as same as the substance abuse. Hence, video game addiction may create some significant changes in cognitive processes, lead to long-term behavioral problems, and adversely affect the natural development of brain (Basak et al. 2008). While some studies argue that playing video games positively affects visual spatial perception, attention, and memory (e.g., Boot et al. 2008; Coltazo et al. 2013), other studies (e.g., Castel et al. 2005; Irons et al. 2011; Murphy and Spencer 2009) indicate playing video games has no or limited effect on cognitive factors (Anderson and Bushman 2001).

Gaming addiction is also categorized based on the contents, namely violent and nonviolent. Today, majority of the popular video games have violent content. One of the well-known results from both neuropsychology and cognitive psychology area is that cognitive functions are strongly related with emotions. Emotional content of the addictive games could differentiate the relationship between game addiction and cognitive processes. Wells (2000) has suggested that individuals show memory and attention bias regarding to the different emotional stimuli matching with their emotional states. Therefore, emotional content could affect cognitive performances of the individuals' both positively and negatively (Wells and Matthews 1994). Based on this hypothesis, being constantly exposed to emotionally violent stimuli, like in violent game addiction, might lead to biases in cognitive processes even if the individuals do not have any cognitive problems. Therefore, the goal of this study is to investigate the effects of playing violent video games on different aspects of cognitive processes such as working memory, object recognition, visual spatial perception, response inhibition, and emotional memory. Violent game addicted group, violent game risk group, and non-players (controls) are compared on above-mentioned cognitive performances using a complex neuropsychological task battery.

1.1.1 Neurobiology of Game Addiction

Brain imaging studies assume that Internet and game addiction share similar mechanisms and changes which take part in brain with those substance related addiction and pathological gambling (Kuss and Griffiths 2012). Results generally suggest that individuals who have symptoms of Internet or game addiction display greater activation in brain regions related to reward, addiction, craving, and emotion during playing the games and presentation of the game cues (Han et al. 2010b; Hoeft et al. 2008). According to that, among addicted Internet users and gamers, especially the nucleus accumbens, amygdala, anterior cingulate, dorsolateral prefrontal cortex, right caudate nucleus, right orbitofrontal cortex, insula, premotor cortex, and precuneus are the brain regions in which increased activations were observed (Ge et al. 2011; Han et al. 2010a, b; Hoeft et al. 2008; Ko et al. 2009). Liu et al. (2010) have stated that Internet addicts' gray matter volume in dorsolateral prefrontal cortex, cerebellum, and supplementary motor region is significantly smaller relative to control groups. Internet addicts are assumed to process sensorimotor and perceptual information better, probably as a result of excessive exposure to applications such as games and leads to increased connectivity between brain regions (Liu et al. 2010).

1.1.2 Video Games and Cognitive Processes

Previous studies about the relationship between video game playing and cognitive functions showed inconsistent results. Those studies could be divided into three groups based on their methods and findings. First group of studies suggest superior cognitive abilities in a number of sensory, perceptual, and attentional domains (Appelbaum et al. 2013). According to that, action video game players respond more rapidly to the relevant stimuli (Dye et al. 2009), track a greater number of items (Green and Bavelier 2006), have better spatial (Boot et al. 2008; Green and Bavelier 2003, 2006) and temporal abilities (Donohue et al. 2010), and are better at task switching (Boot et al. 2008; Cain et al. 2012) relative to non-players. They perform better on working memory (measured by N-back tasks) and detect changes more efficiently (Boot et al. 2008), but do not show enhancements in short-term verbal recall (Cain et al. 2012) or visual short-term memory (Wilms et al. 2013). Second group of studies reports negative effects of engaging in video games frequently, on visuospatial perception, attention, and memory (Boot et al. 2008). On the other hand, third group of studies comparing video game players with non-players state no significant differences between the groups regarding the cognitive processes (e.g., Castel et al. 2005; Murphy and Spencer 2009; Irons et al. 2011).

1.1.2.1 Memory

Previous studies have frequently investigated the role of playing video games on working memory and emotional memory. The differential effects of playing violent video games on various memory performances have become an issue of concern. According to the studies, violent and nonviolent video game experts perform better on short-term memory and working memory tasks (Boot et al. 2008) but they are not different than non-game players on emotional long-term memory (Bowen and Spaniol 2011), whereas they perform worse on verbal memory tasks (Maass et al. 2011).

One of the main conclusions regarding the performance of working memory is that, playing video games might enhance working memory ability of players, since players should store and remember many stimuli at the same time in order to be successful in violent video games (Mahncke et al. 2006). Boot et al. (2008) found that expert video game players had better performance on visual memory task than non-video game players. In their following study (Boot et al. 2010), the participants, who play video games less than 3 h a week, were trained for a new nonviolent video game. They reported that the participants showed superior performance on various memory tasks (e.g., visual, working, and short-term memory) after the training. Recently, Coltazo et al. (2013) observed increased working memory performance measured by video game players compared to non-game players. Conversely, Powers et al. (2013) have failed to find evidence about beneficial effects of playing video games on certain aspects of executive functioning such as multitasking, nonverbal intelligence, task switching, and working memory.

1.1.2.2 Attention and Visuo-Spatial Perception

Playing video games also requires selective attention and concentration. Therefore, performing well on computer games requires being good at those cognitive abilities. Results suggested that when video game players are exposed to a target with distracters during the display, they answer quicker than non-video game players. Boot et al. (2008) study showed that video game players were faster and more accurate in object tracking relative to non-gamers, and game-players detected changes more easily, switching more quickly from one mission to another compared to other groups. Such findings suggested that video game players might be significantly faster in conditions requiring visual search and differentiating the target (Castel et al. 2005; Chrisholm et al. 2010). Green and Bavelier (2003, 2006) compared reaction times of divided and selective attention tasks between video game players and non-players. Video game players were better in detecting at localization of the target and monitoring their attention. Also, they had more control on task switching and temporal attentional processing. This superior performance on visual processing tasks was assumed to be a consequence of changes in the fundamental characteristics of the visual system. Feng et al. (2007) also used a training program and observed participants' improvement on the spatial attention performance. On the other hand, Irons et al. (2011) compared video game players and non-players using Erikson flanker task, however, did not find any significant differences between the groups on processing irrelevant peripheral stimuli. Similarly Ravenzwaaij et al. (2014) reported that playing excessive video games did not increase speed of the information processing during simple perceptual tasks. However, it is still unclear if there are improvements in attentional capabilities as a result of excessive game playing which might increase higher-order processing and cognitive control mechanisms.

1.1.2.3   Inhibition

Inhibition refers to the ability to sustain goal directed information processing in the face of distraction. With regard to the effects of video games on response inhibition, Decker and Gay (2011) have stated that although violent video game players had more difficulty in response inhibition compared to non-players, they showed better reaction time and they had the ability to discriminate targets from distracters. Similarly, Coltazo et al. (2013) observed faster reactions during the N-back task of the video game players compared to controls but there was no difference between two groups on inhibitory control conditions. They concluded that playing video games could be related to enhancements in working memory but not action inhibition. Bailey et al. (2010) reported no differences between high and low gamers in terms of Stroop interference effect and conflict adaptation effect, whereas they found that proactive inhibition was negatively affected by video game experience but reactive inhibition did not. In contrast, Littel et al. (2012) stated that video game players might have a deficiency in response inhibition. In their study, video game players displayed faster reaction times than non-video game players but they also made more errors. As well as it is seen in the other type of addictions (e.g., substance-related addictions), game addiction is assumed to result in poor inhibition, poor error processing and high impulsivity (Kuss and Griffiths 2012). Likewise, Irvine et al. (2013) mentioned that video game-addicted individuals are more impulsive, give premature responses, and prefer immediate rewards even if the delayed reward is more satisfactory.

As a summary, a great deal of studies mentioned the associations between video game playing and improvements in cognitive processes. However, recent behavioral findings suggest that Internet and game addiction leads to problems in impulse control, behavioral inhibition, working memory, and attentional capabilities. Whereas some skills are clearly open to improvements as a result of an extensive involvement with the technology (e.g., integration of perceptual information into brain, hand-eye coordination), disadvantages should not be ignored. Moreover some common methodological differences should be addressed in interpreting the controversial results. First problem is that, various cognitive tasks and/or tests have been used in different studies. Second and more important problem is the lack of accepted inclusion and exclusion criteria regarding the addicted group. Thus homogeneity of participants either within or between the studies becomes a problem because of the difficulty in creating neuropsychological profile of addicted individuals. We used three different measures (hours of playing video game per week, Game Addiction Symptoms List, and Game Addiction Scale) while creating the groups in order to control that problem and to be able to see the cognitive differences between the game addicted, risk, and control groups. Therefore, the present study has two main objectives. First one is to reveal the possible relationships between violent game addiction and different cognitive abilities. Second one is to investigate any differences in terms of the cognitive performances of the individuals among three different groups.

1.2 Method

1.2.1 Participants

The current study was carried out with 98 participants (44 female; 54 male; 18–31 years; $M = 22.47$; $SD = 3.09$). Majority of the participants ($n = 84$; 85.7 %) had undergraduate degree, and 14.3 % ($n = 14$) of participants had graduate degree at the time of testing. Participants were separated into three groups (namely addicted, risk, and control) based on the time they spend for violent game playing (per week), DSM-based pathological game addiction symptoms (Gonnerman and Lutz 2011), and their scores on the Game Addiction Scale developed by Lemmens et al. (2009). All the participants in this study were right-handed, had normal or corrected-to-normal vision, and had no history of neurological, psychological, or memory diseases.

Game-addicted group consisted of 41 participants with mean age of 21.98 ($SD = 3.021$). For this group, the first criterion was playing violent video games more than 16 h/week ($M = 41.95$; $SD = 22.87$; min. 20 h, max. 130 h), the second criterion was reporting more than three symptoms on the Pathological Game Addiction Symptoms List (Gonnerman and Lutz 2011), and the last criterion was obtaining more than 55 total score ($M = 61.27$; $SD = 14.51$) on the Game Addiction Scale (Lemmens et al. 2009). Risk group consisted of 25 students (age $M = 21.36$; $SD = 3.21$). For this group, the first criterion was playing violent video games for 5–16 h a week ($M = 11.32$; $SD = 3.91$), the second criterion was reporting 1 or 2 symptoms on DSM-based Game Addiction Symptoms List (Gonnerman and Lutz 2011), and the last criterion was obtaining total score between 38 and 54 ($M = 37.96$; $SD = 14.2$) on the Game Addiction Scale. Finally control group consisted of 32 participants (age $M = 23.97$; $SD = 2.57$). For this group, the first criterion was not having any experience with any type of video games, the second criterion was obtaining a less than 37 total score ($M = 28.25$; $SD = 3.55$) on the Game Addiction Scale, and the last criterion was reporting no symptoms on the Game Addiction Symptoms List.

1.2.2   Materials

1.2.2.1   Game Addiction Symptoms List

Game Addiction Symptoms List comprised of the pathological gambling symptoms according to DSM-IV (Gonnerman and Lutz 2011). The word "gambling" was replaced with the word "gaming" in the sentences and the sentences have been transformed to "yes" or "no" questions. Adaptation of the list into Turkish culture was completed by Arslan-Durna (2015) and Başer (2015). The list consists of 16 items. The scores that could be obtained from the list range from 0 to 16.

1.2.2.2   Game Addiction Scale

Game Addiction Scale was developed by Lemmens et al. (2009) in order to measure the degree of game addiction. The scale has 21 items with seven factors, which are salience, tolerance, mood modification, relapse, withdrawal, conflict, and problems. Participants give their responses on a 5-point Likert scale from 1 (never) to 5 (very often). Internal consistency of the scale has been reported with range from 0.80 to 0.94. Adaptation of the scale into Turkish culture was completed by Arslan-Durna (2015) and Başer (2015). Participants could obtain a minimum score of 21 and maximum score of 105 on the scale. High scores indicate high levels of game addiction.

1.2.2.3   Working Memory Task

The task was adapted from Harkin and Kessler (2009). It consisted of three phases. The stimuli were capital letters and were presented against a gray back-ground within a 2 (columns) by 3 (rows) matrix covering an area of 300×420 pixels. In the first phase, a 1000-ms fixation cross was shown and four letters were presented randomly in four of the six possible locations. Participants had 1000 ms to encode the identity and the location of each letter. After 500 ms, the probe-1 question requested the location of a specific letter in the second phase. Participants indicated the location via mouse and were instructed that they had little time to answer (2000 ms). In the third phase, whether the probe-1 letter had or had not been part of the encoded set created resolvable versus misleading (irresolvable) trials. In baseline condition, probe-1 was omitted to measure working memory performance on the primary task under ideal conditions. A 500-ms inter-stimulus interval separated probe-1 and probe-2. Since baseline trials did not include the intermediate probe-1, a gray screen was shown for 5500 ms between encoding and probe-2 (equaling the ISI between encoding and probe-2 on the other trial types). Probe-2 was the actual memory test for each trial and required participants to indicate if a letter was correctly located with respect to the originally encoded set (2000 ms). In all of the trials the probe-2 letter had been a part of encoded set in terms of identity while the probe location was correct only on 50 % of the trials. Finally, a scale was displayed prompting participants to indicate their degree of confidence in their probe 2 response (6 levels: 1 = totally certain to 6 = totally uncertain).

1.2.2.4   Object Recognition Task

The task was adapted from Arslan-Durna (2015) and Başer (2015), which consisted of two phases. In the first phase, 15 unfamiliar geometric shapes were shown one at a time in the middle of the computer screen against a gray back-ground. Participants had 1000 ms to encode and learn the shapes. After every shape presented, participants were given a 4 (columns) by 4 (rows) matrix, which boxes filled with 15 distractor shapes and one target shape. Participants were asked to indicate the target shape by using the mouse as quickly as possible in 2000 ms. Then 49 shapes were presented within a 7 (columns) by 7 (rows) matrix and the participants were asked to indicate the target shapes which they have seen previously by using the mouse among them. There is no time limit in this phase. The task lasted about 10 min. High response accuracy and short reaction time indicated higher performance on the object recognition task.

1.2.2.5   Visual Spatial Memory Task

The visual spatial memory task which was adapted from Slotnick and Schacter (2004, 2006) consisted of 40 nonsense shapes. Shapes were generated by using custom software written in MATLAB (The MathWorks Inc.), which were comprised of four pseudo-randomly generated Bezier curves each with end-points on adjacent sides of a bounding square and they had an edge length of 5.5° of visual angle (Slotnick and Schacter 2004, 2006). In the first phase, shapes were presented for 2000 ms with an intertrial interval of 1000 ms on a black computer screen divided by a white line in the middle. Participants were instructed to remember each shape and its spatial location (left or right side of the screen), while always maintaining fixation at the central cross at a time for 1000 ms. In the second phase (recall), same 40 nonsense shapes were presented in different order, and participants were instructed to remember each shape and its spatial location, while always maintaining fixation at the central cross. During this phase, participants had to click on left button of the mouse whenever a shape was presented in the same place than the previous phase, or right button of the mouse whenever a shape was presented in a different place than the previous phase. Duration of the presentation of each shape was 2000 ms. For each participant, a practice section was carried out before the experiment.

1.2.2.6   Response Inhibition Task

The Go/No-Go task was used as a response inhibition measurement. In this study, the Go/No-Go task involved the presentation of letters, one at a time on a screen, for a period of 75 ms, with an inter-stimulus interval of 925 ms. Fifty percent of the stimuli was "X," and the other 50 % was other capital letters randomly selected from the remainder of the alphabet. "X" and "non-X" stimuli were presented in random order. There were two types of Go/No Go task. In the "Respond to X" task, the subject was instructed to press the button when an "X" is presented, and refrain from pressing for all other letters. In the "Respond to non-X" task, the subject was instructed to refrain from pressing for X, and to press for all other letters. Both Go/No-Go tasks were presented in epochs of 20 s duration. Each Go/No-Go epoch was preceded by a 5-s instruction epoch, and followed by a 20-s rest epoch. During instruction epochs, the instruction "Press for X" or "Press for all letters except X" was presented on the screen. During rest epochs, the word "RAHATLAYINIZ" ("Rest" in English) was presented, and the subject was not required to make any motor response. Within the scanning session, there were five "Respond to X," and five "Respond to non-X" epochs, presented in a counterbalanced order. In this task, response times and accuracy scores for Go and No-Go phases were calculated. Individuals who had shorter reaction times in Go trials and more accurate responses in No-Go trials were considered to conduct response inhibition more effectively (Hirose et al. 2012).

1.2.2.7   Emotional Memory Task

A word list was used to assess emotional memory. Sixty violent (e.g., dangerous) and 68 nonviolent (e.g., peaceful) adjectives were chosen as target words from Turkish Word Frequency Dictionary (Göz 2003). The task consisted of three phases. In the first phase, 20 violent and 24 nonviolent words were shown randomly to the participants for 2000 ms. In this phase, participants were asked to learn the presented words on the screen which they will be asked later. In the second phase, a stem completion test was used, and the participants were shown first and third letters of each word (e.g., D_N_____ for the word DANGEROUS) one by one and asked to complete the word. After that, they were asked to indicate how confident they are of their answers using a 6-point Likert-type scale from 1 "not at all" to 6 "extremely strong." In the third phase, 44 previously shown words (20 violent, 24 nonviolent) were presented to the participants with 20 violent and 20 nonviolent new words. All 80 words, except the first and last 2 constant positive words, were presented randomly for 2000 ms. As a part of the classical recognition paradigm, participants were asked to evaluate whether they have seen the presented word previously. In the last phase, participants were requested to indicate how confident they are of their answers using a 6-point Likert-type scale from 1 "not at all" to 6 "extremely strong." Response time, accuracy scores, and the level of confidence rates were calculated. The first and last two words at recall and recognition phases were positive and were not used during statistical analyses in order to control primacy and recency effects.

1.2.3 Procedure

The study was conducted following the approval of the ethics committee at the University. At first, individuals filled out the surveys that inquire about the frequency of playing video games per week and the most frequent games played in general. Based on the information they have given, individuals who match with the inclusion criteria were contacted via phone and those who seem appropriate and accepted to participate to the study were invited. Before the experiment, all participants were given detailed information about the procedure and they were requested to read and to sign the consent form. The experiment was completed in one session separately for each participant in a quiet laboratory room using an IBM compatible 15 in. computer running Windows XP. A comprehensive cognitive battery including working memory, visual spatial memory, emotional memory, response inhibition, and object recognition tasks were given to the participants. Order of the tasks was counterbalanced and detailed instructions and a practice session were given before each task. Administration took approximately 35–40 min for each participant.

1.3 Results

Prior to analyses, the data were screened for missing values, as well as univariate and multivariate outliers (Tabachnick and Fidell 2007). There were no outliers identified as multivariate using Mahalanobis distance with $p < 0.001$, nor univariate using z scores ($|z| \geq 3.30$).

In order to compare neuropsychological task performances of addicted group, risk group, and control group, separate MANOVAs were used. In the analyses group status (three groups) was independent variable, performances, which were measured under each task, were dependent variables. Since multiple analyses were made on the data set, a Bonferroni type adjustment was made for inflated Type 1 error for each comparison separately. For this, α was assigned the value of 0.05 for each p among a set of ps, such that for a set of ps it did not exceed a critical value.

1.3.1 Group Comparisons on Working Memory Task

During the task, number of correct response, incorrect response, reaction time (RT; ms) for correct and RT for incorrect responses of the participants were calculated for probe-1 and probe-2. MANOVA results indicated that group status had

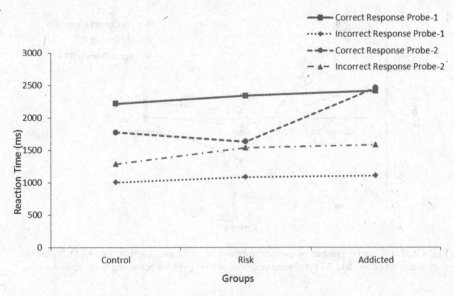

Fig. 1.1 Participants' reaction time during working memory performance according to group status

significant effect on RT for correct response at probe-2, $F(2, 81)=4,64$; $p<0.05$; $\eta_2=0.15$ (see Fig. 1.1). Post-hoc test indicated that addicted group' RT ($M=1800.38$; $SD=295.39$) was significantly higher than control group ($M=1764.86$; $SD=208.78$) and risk group ($M=1567.87$; $SD=244.79$). After the Bonferroni correction, the differences remain significant ($p<0.05$).

1.3.2   Group Comparisons on Object Recognition Task

During the object recognition task, number of correct response, incorrect response, RT (ms) for correct and RT for incorrect responses of the participants were calculated on immediate recall and recognition phases. Result indicated that correct recognition performance of the participants was significantly different, $F(2, 85)=4,99$; $p<0.05$; $\eta_2=0.105$. Recognition performance of the control group ($M=13.66$; $SD=4.88$) was significantly lower than the risk group ($M=17.14$; $SD=4.18$) and addicted group ($M=16.54$; $SD=4.31$). After the Bonferroni correction, the differences were significant ($p<0.05$).

1.3.3   Group Comparisons on Response Inhibition Task

Numbers of correct and incorrect responses and RT for correct and incorrect responses of the participants were calculated for both go and no-go trials. MANOVA results showed that group status's main effect was significant on number of correct

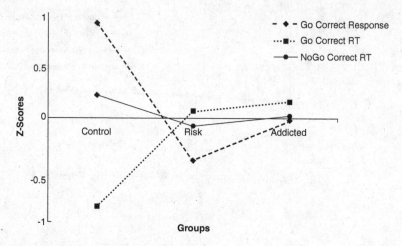

Fig. 1.2 Participants' number of correct response at go phase, reaction time (RT) for correct response at go phase, and RT for correct response at No-Go phase according to group status

response at go phase $F(2, 91)=4.21$; $p<0.05$; $\eta_2=0.107$; RT for correct response at go phase $F(2, 85)=4.99$; $p<0.05$; $\eta_2=0.105$ and RT for correct response at no-go phase $F(2, 85)=3.63$; $p<0.05$; $\eta_2=0.08$ (see Fig. 1.2). Post-hoc comparisons indicated that during go phase, correct response of the control group ($M=49.93$; $SD=2.27$) was significantly higher than the risk group ($M=40.33$; $SD=1.83$), and the addicted group ($M=45.18$; $SD=3.24$). On the other hand RT for both correct and incorrect responses during the go and no-go phases the control group ($M=507.75$; $SD=53.78$; $M=518.47$; $SD=50.02$, respectively) was significantly slower than the risk group ($M=485.66$; $SD=62.29$; $M=493.41$; $SD=61.15$, respectively), and the addicted group ($M=475.91$; $SD=55.51$; $M=490.90$; $SD=59.16$, respectively). After the Bonferroni correction the differences remain significant ($p<0.05$). Group comparisons were also conducted on emotional memory performance and visual-spatial memory performance, but no statistically significant differences were found.

1.4 Discussion

The main goal of the present study was to reveal whether excessive video game playing results in differential changes in certain aspects of cognitive abilities. We compared cognitive performances of violent game-addicted group, risk group, and non-game players (control group) by using a complex neuropsychological test battery, including working memory, object recognition, visual spatial perception, response inhibition, and emotional memory. We found significant effects of excessive video game playing on working memory, object recognition, and response inhibition, whereas no significant differences were found among the groups on emotional memory and visual spatial perception. In details, addicted group showed better performance during object recognition task and their RT was faster during response inhibition (for both go and no-go conditions). On the other hand, during working memory task, addicted group's RT for correct response were significantly slower and their correct responses during response inhibition task were lower compared to risk and control groups.

Video game playing in general requires more than pressing a button at the right time. In order to be successful, game players should monitor and react quickly to the fast moving stimuli, select rapidly the relevant information while filtering out the irrelevant information, and should also avoid inaccurate actions and switch between tasks. Therefore it was consistently hypothesized that more extensive experience with video games could result in increased performance on tasks, which need monitoring and updating of working memory (Coltazo et al. 2013). Contrary, our results have revealed significant group effects on RT for correct responses at probe-2 during working memory task. In this phase, participants were required to indicate if a letter was correctly located with respect to the originally encoded set. According to this, participants in the risk and the addicted groups had higher RTs than control group. Also, video-game addicts did not show any increase in the number of correct responses compared to non-gamers. Also, they were slower while correctly indicating the location of the previously encoded stimuli that indicates that addicted group was slower to recognize previously encoded stimuli compared to other groups. This finding was contradictory to the previous studies, which suggested improvements (e.g., Barlett et al. 2009; Boot et al. 2008; Coltazo et al. 2013; Kearney and Pivec 2005) or no changes (Irons et al. 2011) on working memory performance by individuals experienced in video games.

Since object recognition involves recognition memory, sustained concentration and selective attention, the other hypothesis might be that excessive engagement in video games leads to improvements in object recognition abilities. Expectedly, significant differences in the object recognition performances were observed between the groups. In detail, correct recognition performances of the risk group and the violent video-game addicted group were found better than the control group. This finding was supportive of the Blumberg's (1998) findings in which video game players were found better at focusing on particular cues in the games, which resulted in increased recognition performance. Similar results were found in the studies conducted thereafter. However, these studies generally reported faster reactions by the video game players to targets appeared with distractors in the display (e.g., Castel et al. 2005; Clark et al. 1987; Goldstein et al. 1997).

Previous studies found that video-game practice had little or no effect on object recognition task performance (e.g., Peters et al. 1995), implying that improved performance on visuo-spatial tasks after video-game practice may depend on the kind of spatial abilities needed in the game and in the spatial task (Ogakaki and Frensch 1994). Chrisholm et al. (2010) suggested that experienced video-game players were significantly faster in conditions that require visual searching and classifying the targets. They stated that having experience in video games improves top-down attentional control of individuals. Green and Bavelier (2003, 2006) found consistently that video game players were better in detecting the location of the target and controlling the center of their attention. Such findings supported the idea of video game players having better attentional capacity and effective field of view. On the other hand, even we found better recognition performance in the risk and the addicted groups; their RTs were not different. Our finding suggests improved visuospatial recognition performance by the experienced video-game players. These results are inconsistent with previous studies (e.g., Boot et al. 2008; Donohue et al. 2012).

One possible explanation for the differences between the results could be related to different methods employed by the studies. Previous studies with significant effects of playing video games on working memory and visuo-spatial recognition performance used mostly a practice or a training strategy (e.g., Barlett et al. 2009; Boot et al. 2008). In our study and similar to Irons et al.'s (2011) study, addicted, risk, and control groups were divided based on the self-report of the individuals about their approximate amount of time spent on playing video games per week. Thus, duration of training and time spent for playing video games should be controlled in experimental laboratory studies. Additionally, different from the previous studies, in this study how long individuals engage in violent video games (on-set) was not taken into consideration. In our sample, there might be participants who have been playing violent video games for a short period of time or for years and this could be a factor, which influence the task performance. Finally, the differences (e.g., duration and intensity) between our task and the tasks used in previous studies may account for the discrepancy among results. Therefore, standard methodology should be used in future studies to eliminate this limitation.

We found significant differences among addicted, risk, and control groups on their response inhibition performance. Although individuals in the addicted group showed faster RT during both go and no-go conditions, their correct responses during go condition were lower compared to risk and control groups. Additionally, although it was not significant, higher numbers of incorrect responses for both go and no-go conditions of the addicted group and risk group was remarkable. The results pointed out that experienced video gamers had difficulty in inhibiting their responses compared to non-players. Our results indicated that although experienced video-game players were faster than the non-gamers, it does not increase the number of correct responses. Impulsivity is used to explain maladaptive behaviors including deficits in response inhibition, problem in processing of errors, such as, inability to monitor continuous performance in order to detect and fix errors (Groman et al. 2009; Ridderinkhof et al. 2004). Some impulsive-like behaviors (e.g., drug use) diminished response inhibition and poor error processing contribute to difficulties to resist consumption of a substance and continuation of the behavior despite its negative consequences (Dave et al. 2004; Lubman et al. 2004).

These results might be explained by higher impulsivity and perseveration in excessive video-game players. They could have poor inhibition and error processing abilities when compared to non-gamers. In fact, a number of studies have supported that idea (e.g., Littel et al. 2012; Kuss and Griffiths 2012; Decker and Gay 2011). Similar to our study, Decker and Gay (2011) indicated that video-game players had faster RTs and better ability to discriminate targets from distracters than non-game players, but they showed greater disinhibition than non-players. Additionally, Littel et al. (2012) found that excessive video game players had more errors than controls on no-go trials even they were faster than controls on go trials. They investigated error processing and response inhibition among excessive gamers via ERP recordings. Results showed that addicted gamers had reduced fronto-central event-related negativity (ERN) amplitudes during incorrect trials compared to correct trials and they also had poor error processing similar as in substance dependence and impulse control disorders. The ERN amplitude is associated with perceived accuracy (Scheffers and Coles 2000). Therefore increased errors were interpreted with the reduced awareness and cognitive control regarding the errors by excessive gamers Also, Dong et al. (2010) found that during no-go condition, Internet addicts had lower N2 amplitudes (representing response inhibition-conflict monitoring), higher P3 amplitudes (inhibitory processes-response evaluation), and longer P3 peak latency compared to controls. They stated that Internet addicts had lower activation in conflict detection stage; they were less efficient at information processing and had lower impulse control.

Therefore, these neuroimaging studies indicated that video-game addiction shares some similarities with substance dependence and impulse control disorders in relation to poor inhibition and high impulsivity (Kuss and Griffiths 2012; Treuer et al. 2001). Neuroimaging studies have provided evidence to the idea that excessive gaming might be related to abnormal neurobiological mechanisms in the orbitofrontal cortex and sensory regions, which are associated with impulse control (Park et al. 2010). In their fMRI study Han et al. (2012) found that gaming addicts had more errors as a result of increased impulsiveness.

As conclusion, there have been researches to suggest that video games may lead to some specific benefits, most notably improved visuospatial skills (e.g., Castel et al. 2005; Green and Bavelier 2006). Ferguson and Rueda (2010) mentioned the effect sizes for this research appear to be considerably stronger than for the relationship between violent video games and aggression. Thus, a careful balancing of pros and cons of video games should be undertaken. Our study made important contributions to the literature by extensive knowledge on how cognitive processes are affected by violent gaming addiction. It is difficult to say whether gaming addiction has either negative or positive effects on cognitive processes. But our study indicated that different cognitive functions are affected by gaming in different way. However, the results of the risk group are also remarkable. For many variables, performance of individuals in the risk group was similar (or close) to the addicted group and they were different than the non-players. Therefore, further longitudinal studies are needed in order to observe actual results of gaming addiction on cognitive functions for both risk and addicted groups.

The current study is not without limitations. The first limitation was unequal group sizes. Secondly while categorizing the groups, how long individuals (onset) play video games was not considered. Future research should control these issues in order to attain clear understanding of the relationships between gaming addiction and cognitive processes.

References

Anderson CA, Bushman BJ (2001) Effects of violent video games on aggressive behavior, aggressive cognition, aggressive affect, physiological arousal, and prosocial behavior: a meta-analytic review of the scientific literature. Am Psychol Soc 12:353–359

Appelbaum LG, Cain MS, Darling EF, Mitroff SR (2013) Action video game playing is associated with improved visual sensitivity, but not alterations in visual sensory memory. Atten Percept Psychophys 75:1161–1167. doi:10.3758/s13414-013-0472-7

Arslan-Durna HK (2015) Effects of violent game addiction on executive functions, response inhibition, and emotional memory. Unpublished Master's thesis, Bahçeşehir University Institute of Social Sciences

Bailey K, West R, Anderson CA (2010) A negative association between video game experience and proactive cognitive control. Psychophysiology 47:34–42

Barlett CP, Anderson CA, Swing EL (2009) Video game effects. Confirmed, suspected and speculative: a review of the evidence. Simulat Gaming 40:377–403

Basak C, Boot WR, Voss MW, Kramer AF (2008) Can training in a real time strategy video game attenuate cognitive decline in older adults? Psychol Aging 23:765–777

Başer NF (2015) The effect of violent video games on working memory, object recognition and visuo-spatial perception and its relationships with psychological factors. Unpublished Master's thesis, Bahçeşehir University Institute of Social Sciences

Block JJ (2008) Issues for DSM-V: internet addiction. Am J Psychiatr 165:306–307

Blumberg FC (1998) Developmental differences at play: children's selective attention and performance in video games. J Appl Dev Psychol 19(4):615–624. doi:10.1016/S0193-3973(99)80058-6

Boot WR, Kramer AF, Simons DJ, Fabiani M, Gratton G (2008) The effects of video game playing on attention, memory, and executive control. Acta Psychol 129:387–398

Boot WR, Basak C, Erickson KI, Neider M, Simons DJ, Fabiani M et al (2010) Transfer of skill engendered by complex task training under conditions of variable priority. Acta Psychol 135:349–357

Bowen HJ, Spaniol J (2011) Chronic exposure to violent video games is not associated with alterations of emotional memory. Appl Cogn Psychol 25(6):906–916

Cain MS, Landau AN, Shimamura AP (2012) Action video game experience reduces the cost of switching tasks. Atten Percept Psychophys 74(4):641–647

Castel AD, Pratt J, Drummond E (2005) The effects of action video game experience on the time course of inhibition of return and the efficiency of visual search. Acta Psychol 119(2):217–230

Chrisholm JD, Hickey C, Theeuwes J, Kingstone A (2010) Reduced attentional capture in action video game players. Atten Percept Psychophys 72:667–671

Clark JE, Lanphear AK, Riddick CC (1987) The effects of videogame playing on the response selection processing of elderly adults. J Gerontol 42(1):82–85

Coltazo LS, van den Wildenberg WPM, Zmigrod S, Hommel B (2013) Action video gaming and cognitive control: playing first person shooter games is associated with improvement in working memory but not action inhibition. Psychological Research 77:234–239

Dave S, Gullo MJ, Loxton NJ (2004) Reward drive and rash impulsiveness as dimensions of impulsivity: implications for substance misuse. Addict Behav 29(7):1389–1405

Decker SA, Gay JN (2011) Cognitive-bias toward gaming-related words and disinhibition in World of Warcraft gamers. Comput Hum Behav 27:798–810

Dong G, Lu Q, Zhou H, Zhao X (2010) Impulse inhibition in people with Internet addiction disorder: electrophysiological evidence from a Go/NoGo study. Neurosci Lett 485:138–142

Donohue SE, Woldorff MG, Mitroff SR (2010) Video game players show more precise multisensory temporal processing abilities. Atten Percept Psychophys 72:1120–1129

Donohue SE, Darling EF, Mitroff SR (2012) Links between multisensory processing and autism. Exp Brain Res 222(4):377–387

Dye MW, Green CS, Bavelier D (2009) Increasing speed of processing with action video games. Curr Dir Psychol Sci 18(6):321–326

Feng J, Spence I, Pratt J (2007) Playing action video game reduces gender differences in spatial cognition. Psychol Sci 18:850–855

Ferguson CJ, Rueda SM (2010) The Hitman study: violent video game exposure effects on aggressive behavior, hostile feelings, and depression. Eur Psychol 15(2):99–108

Ge L, Ge X, Xu Y, Zhang K, Zhao J, Kong X (2011) P300 change and cognitive behavioral therapy in subjects with Internet addiction disorder: a 3 month follow up study. Neural Regen Res 6:2037–2041

Gentile DA, Anderson CA (2003) Violent video games: the newest media violence hazard. Media violence and children, pp. 131–152

Goldstein JH, Cajko L, Oosterbroek M, Michielsen M, van Houten O, Salverda F (1997) Video games and the elderly. Soc Behav Personal 25(4):345–352

Gonnerman ME Jr, Lutz GM (2011) Gambling attitudes and behaviors: a 2011 survey of adult Iowan. Center for Social and Behavioral Research, University of Northern Iowa, Cedar Falls

Göz I (2003) Yazılı Türkçe'nin kelime sıklığı sözlüğü (1.basım). Türk Dil Kurumu Yayınları, Ankara

Green CS, Bavelier D (2003) Action video game modifies visual selective attention. Nature 423:534–537

Green CS, Bavelier D (2006) Effects of action video game playing on the spatial distribution of visual selective attention. J Exp Psychol Hum Percept Perform 32:1465–1478

Groman SM, James AS, Jentsch JD (2009) Poor response inhibition: at the nexus between substance abuse and attention deficit/hyperactivity disorder. Neurosci Biobehav Rev 33:690–698. doi:10.1016/j.neubiorev.2008.08.008

Han D, Hwand JW, Renshaw PF (2010a) Bupropion sustained release treatment decreases craving for video games and cue-induced brain activity in patients with Internet video-game addiction. Exp Clin Psychopharmacol 18:297–304

Han D, Kim YS, Lee YS, Min KJ, Renshaw PF (2010b) Changes in cue-induced prefrontal cortex activation with video-game play. Cyberpsychol Behav Soc Netw 13:655–661

Han DH, Lyoo IK, Renshaw PF (2012) Differential regional gray matter volumes in patients with on-line game addiction and professional gamers. J Psychiatr Res 46(4):507–515

Harkin H, Kessler K (2009) How checking breeds doubt: reduced performance in a simple working memory task. Behav Res Ther 47:504–512

Hirose S, Chikazoe J, Watnabe T, Jimura K, Kunimatsu A, Abe O, Ohtomo K et al (2012) Efficiency of Go/No-go task performance implemented in the left hemisphere. J Neurosci 32(26):9059–9065

Hoeft F, Watson CL, Kesler SR, Bettinger KE, Reiss AL (2008) Gender differences in the mesocorticolimbic system during computer game play. J Psychiatry 42:253–258

Irons JL, Remington RW, McLean JP (2011) Not so fast: rethinking the effects of action video games on attentional capacity. Aust J Psychol 63:224–231. doi:10.1111/j.1742-9536.2011.00001.x

Irvine MA, Worbe Y, Bolton S, Harrison NA, Bullmore ET, Voon V (2013) Impaired decisional impulsivity in pathological video gamers. PLoS 8(10), e75914

Kearney P, Pivec M (2005) Recursive loops of game-based learning: a conceptual model, EdMedia: world conference on educational medial and technology in Vancouver, Canada

Kirsch SJ, Olczak PV, Mounts JRW (2005) Violent video games induce an affect processing bias. Media Psychol J 7:239–250

Ko C, Liu G, Hsiao S, Yen J, Yang M (2009) Brain activities associated with gaming urge of online gaming addiction. J Psychiatr Res 43:739–747

Kuss DJ, Griffiths MD (2012) Internet and gaming addiction: a systematic literature review of neuroimaging studies. Brain Sci 2:347–374

Lemmens JS, Valkenburg PM, Peter J (2009) Development and validation of a game addiction scale for adolescents. Media Psychol 12:77–95

Littel M, Berg I, Luijten M, Rooij AJ, Keemink L, Franken IHA (2012) Error processing and response inhibition in excessive computer game players: an event-related potential study. Addict Biol 17:934–947

Liu J, Gao XP, Osunde I, Li X, Zhou SK, Zheng HR, Li LJ (2010) Increased regional homogeneity in Internet addiction disorder: a resting state functional magnetic resonance imaging study. Chin Med J 123:1904–1908

Lubman DI, Yücel M, Pantelis C (2004) Addiction, a condition of compulsive behavior? Neuro-imaging and neuropsychological evidence of inhibitory dysregulation. Addiction 99(2): 1491–1502

Lynch W (1983) Cognitive retraining using microcomputer games and other commercially available software. Paper presented at meeting of the International Neuropsychological Society, Mexico City

Maass A, Klöpper K, Michel F, Lohaus A (2011) Does media use have a short-term impact on cognitive performance? A study of television viewing and video gaming. J Media Psychol 23(2):65–76. doi:10.1027/18641105/a000038

Mahncke HW, Connor BB, Appelman J, Ahsanuddin ON, Hardy JL, Wood RA et al (2006) Memory enhancement in healthy older adults using a brain plasticity-based training program: a randomized, controlled study. PNAS 103(33):12523–12528

Murphy K, Spencer A (2009) Playing video games does not make for better visual attention skills. J Artic Support Null Hypothesis 6:1–20

Ogakaki L, Frensch PA (1994) Effects of video game playing on measures of spatial performance: gender effects in late adolescence. J Appl Dev Psychol 15:33–58

Park HS, Kim SH, Bang SA, Yoon EJ, Cho SS, Kim SE (2010) Altered regional cerebral glucose metabolism in internet game over users: a 18F-fluorodeoxyglucose positron emission tomography study. CNS Spectr 15(3):159–166

Peters M, Laeng B, Latham K, Jackson M, Zaiyouna R, Richardson C (1995) A redrawn Vandenberg and Kuse mental rotations test: different versions and factors that affect performance. Brain Cogn 28:39–58

Powers KL, Brooks PJ, Aldrich NJ, Palladino MA, Alfieri L (2013) Effects of video game on information processing: a meta-analytic investigation. Psychon Bull Rev 20:1055–1079. doi:10.3758/S13423-013-0418-z

Ravenzwaaij D, Boekel W, Forstmann B, Ratcliff R, Wagenmakers E (2014) Action video games do not improve the speed of information processing in simple perceptual tasks. J Exp Psychol 143:1794–1805

Ridderinkhof KR, van den Widenberg WP, Segalowitz SJ, Carter CS (2004) Neurocognitive mechanisms of cognitive control: the role of prefrontal cortex in action selection, response inhibition, performance monitoring, and reward based learning. Brain Cogn 56:129–140

Scheffers MK, Coles MG (2000) Performance monitoring in a confusing world: error-related brain activity, judgments of response accuracy, and types of errors. J Exp Psychol Hum Percept Perform 26:141–151

Slotnick SD, Schacter DL (2004) A sensory signature that distinguishes true from false memories. Nat Neurosci 7:664–672

Slotnick SD, Schacter DL (2006) The nature of memory related activity in early visual areas. Neuropsychologia 44:2874–2886

Sussman S, Sussman AN (2011) Considering the definition of addiction. Int J Environ Res Public Health 8(10):4025–4038

Tabachnick BG, Fidell LS (2007) Using multivariate statistics, 6th edn. Pearson/Allyn & Bacon, Boston

Treuer T, Fábián Z, Füredi J (2001) Internet addiction associated with features of impulse control disorder: is it a real psychiatric disorder? J Affect Disord 66(2):283

Wells A (2000) Emotional disorders and meta cognition: Innovative cognitive therapy. Wiley, Chichester

Wells A, Matthews G (1994) Attention and emotion: A clinical perspective. Laurence Erlbaum Associates, Hillsdale

Wilms IL, Petersen A, Vangkilde S (2013) Intensive video gaming improves encoding speed to visual short-term memory in young male adults. Acta Psychol 142(1):108–118

Chapter 2
Why Games Are Fun? The Reward System in the Human Brain

Mustafa Balkaya and Guven Catak

Abstract Why sugar is sweet? Why sexual activities are pleasurable? Why computer games are fun? Answers to such questions may end up in circular reasoning unless findings from evolutionary biology and neuroscience are not utilized. The brain circuits that determine and modulate the hedonic impact of events and substances are relatively well described and evolutionary theories help us understand the advantages of assigning such a value to "pleasurable" things and activities. The question "Why games are fun," however, seems to require a further understanding of human neuropsychology and evolution because computer games are a very novel part of our lives as a species and quite alien to our past. This concise yet rather dense chapter aims to present a brief introduction and a road map for further reading toward our current scientific understanding of play behavior and how it lays the foundations of the modern phenomena called gaming. Diverse topics ranging from the evolution and adaptive value of play to the neuronal circuits that enable us to derive pleasure from it will be briefly discussed along with examples from experimental studies conducted in humans and animals to elaborate on the "fun" and sometimes addictive nature of games.

Keywords Fun • Brain • Reward systems • Evolution

M. Balkaya, Ph.D. (✉)
Department of Physiology, Bahcesehir University, Istanbul, Turkey
e-mail: mgbalkaya@yahoo.com

G. Catak, Ph.D.
Department of Communication Design, Bahcesehir University Game Lab (BUG),
Bahcesehir University, Istanbul, Turkey
e-mail: guven.catak@comm.bahcesehir.edu.tr

© Springer International Publishing Switzerland 2016
B. Bostan (ed.), *Gamer Psychology and Behavior*, International Series
on Computer Entertainment and Media Technology,
DOI 10.1007/978-3-319-29904-4_2

2.1 Introduction

Let's start with a seemingly banal question, "why sugar is sweet?" An obvious yet unimpressive answer might be: "because it tastes sweet." From a biochemical stand point, it is possible to underlie that all simple carbohydrates are sweet to some degree and table sugar happens to be one of them. Or rather one might state "Substances that bind to sweetness receptors on the tongue are perceived as sweet." As such, depending on the perspective we either find ourselves asking redundant questions and giving redundant answers to a self-evident concept (sweetness) or maybe engage in some sort of circular reasoning. We find ourselves in the exact same kind of situation when we pose questions like; "why fatty foods are rather delicious?," "Why sexual activities are pleasurable?," and "why computer games are fun?" In all such cases, no matter how many different answers we come up with, what remains elusive is the nature of the subjective hedonic component of the experience.

The term sweet does not only refer to the sensation perceived via the stimulation of our taste buds but also contain the subjective hedonic experience that leads us to enjoy and subsequently like the sensory input. Similarly, any pleasurable activity or pleasure in general is never a mere sensation but is always "generated" by the activity of hedonic brain system known as "the reward system." Therefore, no substance, activity, or stimuli is intrinsically pleasurable or rewarding unless the specific brain circuitry is hardwired to react to it and generate the feeling of pleasure. This implies, sensations such as the ones we experience during ingesting sweet substances or sexual activities are "natural" triggers of our reward system. When some fundamental imperatives of Darwinian concept of evolution such as survival and procreation are brought to mind, it is no surprise that nature has selected individuals who experience pleasure from ingesting high calorie foods (sweets) and procreate to have offspring (sexual activity). What remains puzzling is the fact that although it apparently has no evolutionary benefit we still derive pleasure from completing "that" line and watch it disappear in Tetris, finally obtaining the epic gear we longed for in World of Warcraft or watching as our imaginary income increase in an online "idle game." Before further inquiring about the neural circuits and evolutionary legacies that ultimately enable us to derive "fun" from video games let's first take a closer look on play and games.

2.1.1 Play and Game

Recognizing and defining play in daily life may seem trivial, however, it has proven difficult to reach common working definitions for distinct disciplines. Dutch historian Johan Huizinga was one of the first cultural theorists to tackle the task of defining play and its role in culture. In his book Homo Ludens (the playing man), Huizinga defines play as follows: "we might call it a free activity standing quite consciously outside 'ordinary' life as being 'not serious' but at the same time absorbing the player intensely and utterly. It is an activity connected with no material interest, and no profit can be gained by it. It proceeds within its own proper boundaries of time and space according to fixed rules and in an orderly manner. It promotes the formation of social groupings that tend to surround themselves with secrecy and to stress the difference from the common world by disguise or other means." (Huizinga 1970) Throughout the history of academic studies of play, various modifications and alternatives to Huizinga's definitions have been brought forward but his pioneering work and descriptions has remained ever influential. More recently, Burghardt proposed more clear-cut and particularly useful working definitions with five distinct categorical criteria for recognizing play in all species. According to these criteria, a behavior is considered play if it is (1) incompletely functional in the context in which it appears, (2) voluntary, spontaneous, pleasurable, or rewarding, (3) different from other behaviors in form (e.g., exaggerated) or timing (e.g., early in life), (4) repeated but not stereotypic or abnormal and (5) initiated in the absence of severe stress (Burghardt 2010).

Be it humans or animals, observed play behavior can show quite a variation and diversity yet be described in three categories (1) solitary locomotor-rotational play in which solitary individuals display vigorous motor acts that appear to be exaggerated versions of normal locomotors patterns (e.g., somersaulting in monkeys), (2) object play in which an individual is interacting or manipulating and object in a playful manner (e.g., a cat playing with a toy mouse) and (3) social play in which two or more individuals interact with each other in a playful manner (e.g., play fight in dogs) (Graham and Burghardt 2010; Fagen 1981). Needless to say, while still belonging to the above-mentioned categories human play has many higher order "layers." A child running around in a backyard may look as if he is engaged in a sort of solitary locomotion play that may as well be observed in various animals. In fact in his mind he may be pretending to be a dragon flying in a mystical journey. Accordingly, the National Institute of Play describes three distinct categories of play (imaginative and pretend play, storytelling play, creative play) that is generally attributed to human play. In imaginative and pretend play, a person pretends being in imagined locations and situations and participating in invented scenarios and acts within them as in the above-mentioned example. Storytelling play refers to the strictly language-dependent play where adults tell or retell a story to children. Creative play refers to the situations where play and playful activities are used to innovate and create as in the case of advertising agents trying to create a jingle or designers employing playful brainstorming or work to create novel designs and approaches. Depending on the species, observed play can be as simple as some playful locomotor behaviors or an elaborate display of social skills and interactions. At some stage play becomes even more complex and transforms to a game.

In his article What Is a Game, Bernard Suits writes "to play a game is to engage in activity directed toward bringing about a specific state of affairs, using only means permitted by specific rules, where the means permitted by the rules are more limited in scope than they would be in the absence of the rules, and where the sole reason for accepting such limitation is to make possible such activity" (Suits 1967).

Going back to the play definition by Burghardt, we can already see that play behavior is "bringing about a specific state of affairs" since it is incompletely functional in the context in which it appears and different from other behaviors. We would argue that what really distinguishes game from play in Suits definition is his assertion that games initiate a special and specific state that is governed and only made possible by rules. For Eric Zimmerman and Katie Salen "A game is a system in which players engage in an artificial conflict, defined by rules, that results in a quantifiable outcome" (Salen and Zimmerman 2004). This approach marks quantifiable outcome as the second fundamental component of a game. Hence it is possible to define game as play structured by rules and goals.

2.1.2 Evolution of Play

The life on our planet is the product of evolution. Every aspect of every living organism, from its physiology to behavior, has been shaped by the unrelenting "forces" of natural selection. A complex behavior such as play is surely not an exception to this rule. Primates, rodents, ungulates, carnivorans, and elephants display complex play behavior (Graham and Burghardt 2010). Play like behavior is also observed in many diverse phylogenetic groups including mammals, lizards, crustaceans, insects, turtles, frogs, and fishes (Graham and Burghardt 2010; Dapporto et al. 2006; Mather and Anderson 1999; Burghardt 2005). Additionally, animal play can reach such complexity in nonhuman primates; it warrants the definition of imaginary and pretend play or even game. Various reports document imaginary play in chimpanzees and bonobos (Jensvold and Fouts 1993), a game of tag quite similar to that found in human children was observed in captive gorillas. Fascinatingly, animals also play computer games! Captive primates and monkeys were able to play rather complex computer games designed for experimental purposes. In a series of studies investigating the memory performance, chimpanzees were able to interact with a touch screen and complete a memory task. During the task, animals were briefly exposed to a sequence of Arabic numerals which they have to touch in an ascending order after the numerals are concealed (Kawai and Matsuzawa 2000). In another example, monkeys were trained to play video shooting games by manipulating joysticks to shoot bullets at a target. In this computer game that rightfully deserves the name "shooter," monkeys were able to play in single player (monkey vs. computer) or multiplayer (monkey vs. monkey) sessions (Hosokawa and Watanabe 2012).

The fact that a play is observed in many distinct species indicates that it most probably evolved repeatedly and independently in different taxa (Burghardt 2005). Play is so ubiquitous in such a variety of species; many researchers of the field proposed it should be adaptive (i.e., increasing fitness, survival, and reproductive success) rather than being a by-product or spandrel.

Even a brief observation of play (i.e., locomotor play) would lead to the conclusion that play is costly in terms of energy. In addition, attention that can otherwise be directed to survival-related behavior such as foraging, hunting, courtship or avoiding predators is diverted to play. It has been documented that 85 % of American fur seal pups which became sea lion prey were engaged in play when captured (Harcourt 1991). According to life history theory, unless there are substantial compensatory benefits, animals that exhibit costly behaviors in terms of survival, energy, and time will suffer decreases in fitness and evolutionary success (Caro 1988). Therefore, play should have considerable benefits otherwise there would be a very strong selection against it.

Various theories were proposed to explain the possible adaptive function of play but all fall in three major categories: play as physical training, play as social training, and play as cognitive training (Chick 2001). These theories suggest that playful behavior displayed in early life serves as means to train and mature the neural and physiological correlates of adult behaviors and skills that are essential to survival and reproductive success. Adult behaviors that can potentially be honed by play include motor skills required for fighting and predatory skills, skills required for mating, or complex skills required for social behavior (Brownlee 1954; Byers and Walker 1995). In addition, it has been suggested that (especially adult) play can have primarily social benefits such as reducing aggression and promoting cooperative behavior (Bekoff 2001; Pellis and Pellis 2007). Despite the clear line of thought and logic, it has proven difficult to ascertain the adaptive value of play in nonhuman animals. A number of studies failed to find a clear relation between play and specific set of skills. Rate and success in play fights did not predict the ability to win real fights in adulthood in wild meerkats (Sharpe 2005a). Kitten raised in toy enriched environments were no better than kittens that were prevented to play with objects in predatory skills (Caro 1980). Similarly some mammals were able to develop regular social skills even deprived of play (Baldwin and Baldwin 1973) and in wild meerkats social play did not reduce aggression and had no observable effect on group dynamics (Sharpe 2005b, c; Sharpe and Cherry 2003).

On the other hand, growing evidence from laboratory and long-term field studies supports the notion that play has an adaptive value. A field study describes bear cubs that play more as cubs had better survival rates as adults (Fagen and Fagen 2004, 2009). Similarly, an evaluation of field data on yellow baboons reveal that early life play behaviour predicts both early and prospective wellbeing (Pereira and Fairbanks 1993). More recently, it was documented that social dominance in adulthood is related to juvenile play in yellow-bellied marmoths (Blumstein et al. 2013). Rate of social play shows a positive relation with subsequent reproductive success in ground squirrels (Nunes et al. 2004) and feral horses that spend more time playing were having a higher survival rate (Cameron et al. 2008). In controlled laboratory experiments, rats reared in isolation or with non-playful cage partners had difficulty in achieving the appropriate orientation during mounting and showed deficits in sexual behavior (Hard and Larsson 1971). Laboratory rats deprived of play fights were inept at distinguishing threatening from nonthreatening situations and always responded with an exaggerated defensive behavior (Potegal and Einon 1989).

Taken together, there is not enough convincing evidence showing that specific motor, cognitive, and social behaviors are fostered by play; however, a relation between play and individual adaptation appears warranted. (For detailed reviews on evolution of play, see Burghardt 2014 and Fagen 1981.)

At this stage, we can safely assume play confers some adaptive benefits to complex organisms; hence, play behavior is selected through their evolution. Yet we are still not close to understanding the mechanisms or drives why animals or people do play games. It has to be remembered that animals do not act or pursue certain incentives with the knowledge of their beneficial nature. What is the incentive that drives us to play? One must revisit classical psychology theories on incentive and motivation and the first land mark on the road is the concept of reward.

2.2 Reward and Operant Conditioning

Oxford dictionary defines reward as "a thing given in recognition of service, effort, or achievement." In that sense, reward is obviously something pleasant, but not only that, it is a pleasant prize that is received only if a certain behavior is performed. Somewhat in line with that definition, in behavioral psychology jargon, reward is any appetitive stimuli that can alter behavior (i.e., increase its occurrence frequency). This definition does not exclude the hedonic component of reward but rather underlies the fact that rewarding stimuli can alter the behavior of an animal or a person.

Since it is not possible to reliably measure subjective pleasure experienced, the easiest way is to observe the effects of reward on behavior. A particularly well-established protocol to study the effects of rewarding stimuli on animal behavior is "operant conditioning." Mainly established by the pioneering work of American psychologist B. F. Skinner, operant conditioning is a learning process in which behavior is altered as a result of its consequences. In its simplest form, animals are isolated in an experimental box that contains a lever which animal can press simply by accident. Whenever the lever is pressed, the animal receives a food pallet or some sweet treat. With enough repetition, the animal learns the association between the behavior (pressing the lever) and outcome (receiving food) and quickly increases the frequency of the behavior. In this context, the food is the reward and a reinforcing stimulus since it has successfully reinforced (by increasing its frequency) a certain behavior (Staddon and Cerutti 2003).

Operant conditioning has been widely and extensively used in behavioral psychology research. A major breakthrough achieved via operant conditioning was the discovery that when electrodes placed in certain regions of the brain were activated via the lever in the operant conditioning apparatus, animals' behavior was altered as in reward administration. In their classical paper Olds and Milner describe that rats tend to return to the portion of the test apparatus where they received electrical stimulation to the septal area of the brain. When presented with a lever that would trigger short pulse trains of electrical stimulation to the same area, animals quickly learned to execute vigorous lever pressing. Olds and Milner concluded that the stimulation was rewarding and electrical stimulation to certain regions of the brain can serve as operant reinforcer (Olds and Milner 1954). Depending on the area of electrode placement, the rewarding properties of the electrical stimulation could be so potent that animals would forego other activities including feeding and drinking.

Further studies in rats and humans enabled researchers to map such areas more thoroughly. Today, we have quite an extensive understanding of the anatomical areas involved in reward processing and reward-dependent learning.

2.3   The Reward System

Our sensory perceptions, feeling, emotional states, and consciousness are a product of the activity, interaction, and emergent properties of the complex neuronal networks and the connectome of our central nervous system. Similarly, our subjective hedonic experiences are created by a particular network of brain structures called the reward system. Various cells of the brain respond to reward; however, brain circuits from the cortex to the basal ganglia constitute the core of the reward system. Electrical stimulation and pharmacological manipulation studies indicate dopaminergic neurons in the nucleus accumbens (NAc), and the ventral tegmental area plays a central role in reward processing. The anatomy and physiology of the reward system is rather complex and beyond the scope of this chapter. Briefly, key brain regions include the ventral striatum, the ventral pallidum, the anterior cingulate cortex, and the orbitofrontal cortex (OFC). Other structures such as amygdala, thalamus, hippocampus, and dorsal prefrontal cortex take part in reward system regulation (for a detailed review, see Haber and Knutson 2010).

With the development of noninvasive techniques such as functional magnetic resonance imaging (FMRI), human studies on reward system gained significant pace. Findings from FMRI studies in the last two decades indicate that OFC-amygdala-NAC reward circuit "responds" to a diverse set of stimuli. Basic rewarding stimuli such as water, fruit juice, appetitive smells, (Haber and Knutson 2010; Berns et al. 2001; O'Doherty et al. 2001) sexual stimuli and sexual behavior induce changes in the activity of the reward circuit (Arnow et al. 2002; Komisaruk et al. 2004). Conditioned rewards (such as money) that are not initially reward but acquire their reward status through learning also alter the activity of the similar circuitry (Knutson et al. 2000). Social interactions, pleasant touch, and seeing beautiful faces also became pleasurable through the activity of the same structures (Rilling et al. 2002; Hamann and Mao 2002; Rolls et al. 2003). Although anatomical substrates of reward processing are well understood, the exact roles those structures play is yet to be fully elucidated. (For a detailed review, see McClure et al. 2004.)

2.3.1 Intrinsic Rewards and Motivation

As discussed above, certain rewards such as food and sexual contact confer evolutionary benefit to the individual so it is only natural that seeking and obtaining such rewards are pleasurable. Such rewards are therefore called primary rewards. However, both animals and humans do pursue rewards that—at a first glance—do not seem to increase individuals' bodily resilience or likelihood of passing on their genes to the next generations. Monetary gains are a classic example of such secondary rewards. It should be noted however that secondary rewards derive their value from primary rewards and become rewarding due to the learned associations between them. In both primary and secondary rewards, the reward is external as in something to be obtained from the environment. Play behavior do not lead to any tangible external reward that will reinforce the behavior. Therefore, for such reinforcement to exist there should be internal rewards. When a reward originates from within the person doing the activity, it is called an internal reward.

Skinner's Operant theory proposes that all behaviors are motivated by rewards and intrinsically motivated behaviors are the ones which activity itself is the reward. From human perspective, intrinsic motivation is defined as the doing of an activity for its inherent satisfaction and exercising one's capacities.

2.3.2 Gaming Stimuli as Reward

Any gamer would certainly testify they are getting pleasure from games but in terms of the brain networks do game stimuli really activate the very same reward pathways that natural rewards do? In 1998, Koepp demonstrated dopamine release in ventral striatum during a tank simulation game play. Additionally, the amount of dopamine released during game play was correlated with the subjects in game performance (Koepp et al. 1998). Using FMRI, activation of Nucleus accumbens during game play was shown (Hoeft et al. 2008). Interestingly, in the same study, males showed greater activation and functional connectivity compared to females in the mesocorticolimbic reward system. While playing a shooter game, Caudate nucleus activation was suppressed during a failure (killed by an opponent) and striatal activation was stronger in instances of success. Players did not show any increase in reward circuit activity during violent events showing that success is rewarding rather than acts of violence (Mathiak et al. 2011). When played against a human, opponent reward system activity was drastically different. When playing versus human opponents instead of a computer AI, test subjects exhibited greater activation in ventral and dorsal striatum and ventromedial prefrontal cortex (vmPFC) (Katsyri et al. 2013). Taken together, experimental studies indicate that playing computer games engage the dopaminergic brain reward circuit, particularly the striatum and the vmPFC. Despite its virtual nature, the rewards that we get from computer games are not any less real at the neurobiological level.

Table 2.1 Sixteen basic human motivators

Motivator	Object of desire
Power	Influence
Curiosity	Knowledge
Independence	Self-reliance
Acceptance	Be part of group
Order	Organization
Saving	Collecting things
Honor	Loyalty to one's parents, community
Idealism	Social justice, equity
Social contact	Companionship
Family	Raising your own children
Status	Social standing
Vengeance	Competition, getting even
Romance	Sex and beauty
Eating	Food
Phyical activity	Exercising the body
Tranquility	Emotional calm

2.3.3 "Gaming Literature" on Why We Play

As computer games gradually started becoming a prominent part of our daily lives, gaming behavior started to draw the attention of the scientific community. Researchers from various disciplines have been studying the very same question we pose in this chapter: why games are fun and why we play them. The conclusion that the "gaming literature" reaches can actually be summarized (albeit with significant simplification) as: "we play games because games trigger the very same motivations and offer the same "objects of desire" that we experience and pursue in our "real" daily life.

To see the overlap between our daily and in game motives the 16 basic human motivators and their objects of desire described by Dr. Steven Reiss can be examined (Table 2.1) (Reiss 2000). Going through those motivators we already start to discover the components of fun in video games. It has to be kept in mind that games come in a huge variety. There are extremely simple games such as Pong were players are just trying to prevent a ball from exiting the game field while competing against an AI opponent and extremely complex games such as Second Life where players are in an online virtual world with millions of regular players constructing and living a second life of their—virtual—own. With the exception of eating, it is quite trivial to give game examples that would incite one or more of the motivators listed. If you are motivated by "curiosity" and "saving" and you desire to explore and collect things, point-and-click adventure games are definitely your thing with their huge inventories. Or if you want power to influence people, you should play Civilization where you are the eternal ruler of a particular folk. Tetris might be particularly attractive if you are seeking order. Well for family, you can play SIMS or second life.

Jon Radoff takes this concept further in his book Game On and matches the list of 16 basic human motivators (except eating) with a list of 42 things that humans report enjoying in computer games (Radoff 2011). The list by Radoff gives a glimpse of the diversity of fun elements games can offer. Each individual fun element can stir one or more of our natural motivations which indicate that even in simple games more than one of our natural tendencies find a medium to express itself (Table 2.2).

The complexity of today's most popular massively multiplayer online role-playing games (MMORPG) where it is possible to be a hero, collect items, socialize, improve your character, overcome the obstacles by recognizing patterns definitely offer a "playground" for our intrinsic motivations. The fact that millions of people from different countries with different age and socioeconomic groups do participate in those vast virtual words is a clear indicator that such games can offer something for everyone.

Jon Radoff also mentions that most of those fun elements are attached with the five happiness factors described in the P.E.R.M.A. model on an emotional level. First proposed by Martin Seligman as a part of his well-being theory, the P.E.R.M.A. model describes five universal categories of experiences that constitute the foundations of a "good" and fulfilling life. These categories are as follows (Seligman 2011):

Positive emotions refer to a wide range of positive feelings such as excitement, joy, happiness, pride, and satisfaction.

Engagement or flow is the state of being involved and immersed in an activity of interest.

Relationships refer to our social interactions with other people. Not only romantic relations but also any kind of bond that we share with other individuals or social groups falls under this category.

Meaning is the feeling of belonging to something bigger and having a satisfactory answer to the question "Why." Meaning is both the source and result of having a purpose in life.

Accomplishments are our life goals we try to reach. Also the pursuit of mastery and success...

If we follow Radoff's perspective on gamer motivations and their close relation to P.E.R.M.A., then we have to conclude: Games offer us means to freely and safely act upon our motivations in a medium that is inherently rigged to please us (unlike real life), with just the right amount of uncertainty (to further boost our reward system) and a touch of challenge and effort our motivations meet their fulfillment thus giving us P.E.R.M.A. experiences and a "better" life.

However, it is not clear if this line of thought perfectly resembles the situation in real life. More research is needed to evaluate if gamers report higher happiness levels or life fulfillment in the long run. A survey among gamers show longer hours of online gaming is related to higher scores of depression and social phobia (Wei et al. 2012). It has to be noted that this relation might be a coping mechanism for people with more severe depressive symptoms. Likewise, another study found

Table 2.2 Jon Radoff's 42 fun things

Motivator/fun elements	Power	Curiosity	Independence	Acceptance	Order	Saving	Honor	Idealism	Social contact	Family	Status	Vengeance	Romance	Physical activity	Tranquility
#1: Recognizing patterns	X	X			X										
#2: Collecting	X				X	X					X				
#3: Finding unexpected treasure	X					X					X				
#4: Achieving a sense of completion	X		X		X										X
#5: Gaining recognition for achievements				X					X		X				
#6: Creating order out of chaos					X										X
#7: Customizing virtual worlds			X						X		X				
#8: Gathering knowledge		X							X		X				
#9: Organizing groups of people					X				X	X	X		X		
#10: Noting insider references				X					X						
#11: Being the center of attention	X										X		X		
#12: Experiencing beauty and culture					X								X		X
#13: Romance							X			X			X		
#14: Exchanging gifts				X				X		X			X		

(continued)

Table 2.2 (continued)

Motivator/fun elements	Power	Curiosity	Independence	Acceptance	Order	Saving	Honor	Idealism	Social contact	Family	Status	Vengeance	Romance	Physical activity	Tranquility
#15: Being a hero	X		X				X	X	X		X	X	X		
#16: Being a villain	X		X									X			
#17: Being a wise old man	X		X	X			X			X	X				
#18: Being a rebel	X		X		X				X		X	X	X		
#19: Being a ruler	X				X		X			X	X		X		
#20: Pretending to live in a magical place		X						X					X		X
#21: Listening to a story		X							X						
#22: Telling stories	X			X							X				
#23: Predicting the future					X										
#24: Competition	X	X			X						X	X		X	
#25: Psychoanalyzing	X	X													
#26: Mystery		X											X		
#27: Mastering a skill	X		X											X	
#28: Exacting justice and revenge	X										X	X	X		
#29: Nurturing							X			X	X		X		
#30: Excitement														X	
#31: Triumph over conflict	X											X			
#32: Relaxing															X

#33: Experiencing the Freakish or Bizarre	X											X
#34: Being silly		X										
#35: Laughing		X										
#36: Being scared			X									
#37: Strengthening a family relationship			X		X							
#38: Improving one's health				X								
#39: Imagining a connection with the past					X	X			X			
#40: Exploring a world	X							X				
#41: Improving society	X						X					
#42: Enlightenment	X	X						X				

higher rates of depressive tendencies, low self-esteem, and problematic gaming behavior in MMORPG players compared to online shooter players (Stetina et al. 2011). To prevent doing injustice to games and adding to the already existing stigma we must note that almost all similar studies in the literature focus on gaming addiction and problematic gaming behavior. We are of the opinion that depressive symptoms and other related problems are the cause of excessive and problematic gaming rather than games being the reason. In line with that argument several studies report elevations in mood, relaxation, and reduced anxiety with game play (Russoniello et al. 2009; Ryan et al. 2006). Additionally, computer game play seems to have significant social benefits. Evidence from longitudinal and experimental studies shows that playing prosocial games that reward cooperation is related to prosocial behaviors in daily life (Gentile et al. 2009). Despite the widespread prejudice, players who play violent games that involve cooperative play are more likely to exhibit helpful behavior both in game and real life (Ferguson and Garza 2011). Similarly, playing cooperative violent computer games decreased players' access to aggressive cognitions (Schmierbach 2010). (For a detailed review on benefits of computer games, see Granic et al. 2014.)

To further understand individual reasons of gaming we can refer to Richard Bartle's classis essay "Hearts, Clubs, Diamonds, Spades: Players Who Suit MUDs" where he describes four main player types (Bartle 1996):

- *Achievers* who are proud of their formal status in the game's built-in level hierarchy and how short a time they took to reach it.
- *Explorers* who are proud of their knowledge of the game's finer points, especially if we knew players treat them as founts of all knowledge.
- *Socializers* who are proud of their friendships, their contacts and their influence.
- *Killers* are proud of their reputation and of their oft-practiced fighting skills.

Just like the overlap between the in game motivations and motivations of daily life we see something quite familiar in those character types. One can simply take such player types out of the game context and match them to the characters and persona we see in our everyday life.

2.4 Conclusion

Play behavior exists in a wide range of species and it most probably evolved repeatedly and independently in different taxa. The fact that evolution favored play behavior testifies for its adaptive value. The benefits of play for learning motor as well as social skills are pretty self-evident to any parent and educator. However, when it comes to playing computer games, public perception is quite mixed regarding their effects on our youth. While the beneficial aspects of computer gaming on several different motor, sensory, and cognitive skills are gaining attention and recognition, there is still a sort of stigma against computer games and gaming, framing it as a waste of time keeping people from productive work and even rendering them prone to violence. In the midst of such controversy, computer games are becoming more popular by day.

Regardless of their nature, rewards alter the activity of the very same circuitry in our brain. Recent FMRI studies show that computer game can serve as potent reward. Being praised by a raid partner in a MMORPG can be as pleasing as a pat at the back from a colleague at work. Finally, obtaining an epic gear in your favorite game may be as rewarding as your next birthday present. Despite being relatively novel, computer games are actually not drastically different than the games we used to play. They are more sophisticated thus more of our daily motivations can be projected upon them.

Apparently, the moment we comfortably interact with virtuality, virtual becomes "real." Through interaction, any virtual entity first becomes a tool (as in a hammer or a tennis racket) then the tool becomes a bodily extension. Depending on its complexity and the richness of the virtual medium that it is present in, the extension can become incorporated to the body image to such extent that it becomes a duplicate of the body, the person, and his intrinsic motivations. Therefore, we would argue that the question "why computer games are fun" is somewhat redundant. The real quest is to thoroughly understand why and how we experience, process and value pleasure, fun and joy in the first place. Playing and enjoying computer games is definitely not a peculiar behavioral oddity. The computer games are fun because playing games are fun. Playing games are fun because we are neurally and evolutionarily hard wired to derive pleasure from them. If our civilization and culture continues in its current pace in providing us more free time, better interaction with computers, enriched virtuality, and less meaning in the real world, more time will be spent by more people seeking fun, happiness, meaning, and (for some) refuge in computer games.

Computer games and virtually is yet to reach its full potential and it is quite difficult to envision what lies ahead in the long run. What seems to be certain is they will become more realistic, more sophisticated, more pervasive, more creative, and more fun. Therefore, a "generation of gamers" whose life will be drastically shaped and even defined by gaming culture are about to make debut. Will future games become a terribly addictive "reward trap" depriving many of the will or chance to do anything meaningful in life or will they open novel possibilities that we cannot even dream of at the moment. We can only wait and see.

As a final word, we would like you to imagine a likely event that took place in our distant past thousands of years ago even before Homo sapiens walked the earth. A hominid sitting at some corner of a damp and dark cave, playing with some dry branches … Maybe he was an eccentric among his peers; just a "low rank" primate in the group. Perhaps, he was well liked by males and females alike because of his playful nature. As he was vigorously rubbing those dry sticks of wood and grass together almost obsessively hundreds of times who knows what others thought of him. Did they think he was wasting his time? Did they get upset because he was not doing anything useful? Regardless of what his group thought of him then, today should we salute him as Prometheus, the bringer of fire.

References

Arnow BA, Desmond JE, Banner LL, Glover GH, Solomon A, Polan ML et al (2002) Brain activation and sexual arousal in healthy, heterosexual males. Brain 125:1014–1023

Baldwin JD, Baldwin JI (1973) The role of play in social organization: comparative observations on squirrel monkeys (Saimiri). Primates 14:369–381

Bartle R (1996) Hearts, clubs, diamonds, spades: players who suit MUDs [Online]. Available from: http://mud.co.uk/richard/hcds.htm

Bekoff M (2001) Social play behaviour: cooperation, fairness, trust, and the evolution of morality. J Conscious Stud 8:81–90

Berns GS, McClure SM, Pagnoni G, Montague PR (2001) Predictability modulates human brain response to reward. J Neurosci 21:2793–2798

Blumstein DT, Chung LK, Smith JE (2013) Early play may predict later dominance relationships in yellow-bellied marmots (Marmota flaviventris). Proc Biol Sci 280:20130485

Brownlee A (1954) Play in domestic cattle in Britain: an analysis of its nature. Br Vet J 110: 48–68

Burghardt GM (2005) The genesis of animal play: testing the limits. MIT Press, Cambridge

Burghardt GM (2010) Defining and recognizing play. Oxford University Press, Oxford

Burghardt GM (2014) A brief glimpse at the long evolutionary history of play. Anim Behav Cogn 1:90–98

Byers JA, Walker C (1995) Refining the motor training hypothesis for the evolution of play. Am Nat 146:25–40

Cameron EZ, Linklater WL, Stafford KJ, Minot EO (2008) Maternal investment results in better foal condition through increased play behavior in horses. Anim Behav 76:1511–1518

Caro TM (1980) Effects of the mother, object play, and adult experience on predation in cats. Behav Neural Biol 29:29–51

Caro TM (1988) Adaptive significance of play: are we getting closer? Trends Ecol Evol 3:50–54

Chick G (2001) What is play for? Sexual selection and the evolution of play. Play Cult Stud 3(1):3–25

Dapporto L, Turillazzi S, Palagi E (2006) Dominance interactions in young adult paper wasp (Polistes dominulus) foundresses: a playlike behavior? J Comp Psychol 120:394–400

Fagen RM (1981) Animal play behavior. Oxford University Press, Oxford

Fagen R, Fagen J (2004) Juvenile survival and benefits of play behaviour in brown bears, Ursus arctos. Evol Ecol Res 6:89–102

Fagen R, Fagen J (2009) Play behaviour and multi-year juvenile survival in free-ranging brown bears, Ursus arctos. Evol Ecol Res 11:1053–1067

Ferguson CJ, Garza A (2011) Call of (civic) duty: action games and civic behavior in a large sample of youth. Comput Hum Behav 27:770–775

Gentile DA, Anderson CA, Yukawa S et al (2009) The effects of prosocial video games on prosocial behaviors: international evidence from correlational, longitudinal and experimental studies. Pers Soc Psychol Bull 35(6):752–763

Graham KL, Burghardt GM (2010) Current perspectives on the biological study of play: signs of progress. Q Rev Biol 85:393–418

Granic I, Lobel A, Engels RC (2014) The benefits of playing video games. Am Psychol 69:66–78

Haber SN, Knutson B (2010) The reward circuit: linking primate anatomy and human imaging. Neuropsychopharmacology 35:4–26

Hamann S, Mao H (2002) Positive and negative emotional verbal stimuli elicit activity in the left amygdala. Neuroreport 13:15–19

Harcourt R (1991) Survivorship costs of play in the South American fur seal. Anim Behav 42:509–511

Hard E, Larsson K (1971) Climbing behavior patterns in prepubertal rats. Brain Behav Evol 4:151–161

Hoeft F, Watson CL, Kesler SR, Bettinger KE, Reiss AL (2008) Gender differences in the mesocorticolimbic system during computer game-play. J Psychiatr Res 42:253–258

Hosokawa T, Watanabe M (2012) Prefrontal neurons represent winning and losing during competitive video shooting games between monkeys. J Neurosci 32:7662–7671

Huizinga J (1970) Homo Ludens: a study of the play element in culture. Temple Smith, London

Jensvold MLA, Fouts RS (1993) Imaginary play in chimpanzees (pan troglodytes). Hum Evol 8:217–227

Katsyri J, Hari R, Ravaja N, Nummenmaa L (2013) The opponent matters: elevated FMRI reward responses to winning against a human versus a computer opponent during interactive video game playing. Cereb Cortex 23:2829–2839

Kawai N, Matsuzawa T (2000) Numerical memory span in a chimpanzee. Nature 403:39–40

Knutson B, Westdorp A, Kaiser E, Hommer D (2000) FMRI visualization of brain activity during a monetary incentive delay task. Neuroimage 12:20–27

Koepp MJ, Gunn RN, Lawrence AD, Cunningham VJ, Dagher A, Jones T, Brooks DJ, Bench CJ, Grasby PM (1998) Evidence for striatal dopamine release during a video game. Nature 393:266–268

Komisaruk B, Whipple B, Crawford A et al (2004) Brain activation during vaginocervical self-stimulation and orgasm in women with complete spinal cord injury. Brain Res 1024:77–88

Mather JA, Anderson RC (1999) Exploration, play and habituation in octopuses (Octopus dofleini). J Comp Psychol 113:333–338

Mathiak KA, Klasen M, Weber R, Ackermann H, Shergill SS, Mathiak K (2011) Reward system and temporal pole contributions to affective evaluation during a first person shooter video game. BMC Neurosci 12:66

McClure SM, York MK, Montague PR (2004) The neural substrates of reward processing in humans: the modern role of FMRI. Neuroscientist 10:260–268

Nunes S, Muecke E-M, Lancaster LT, Miller NA, Mueller NA, Muelhaus J, Castro L (2004) Functions and consequences of play behaviour in juvenile Belding's ground squirrels. Anim Behav 68:27–37

O'Doherty J, Kringelbach ML, Rolls ET, Hornak J, Andrews C (2001) Abstract reward and punishment representations in the human orbitofrontal cortex. Nat Neurosci 4:95–102

Olds J, Milner P (1954) Positive reinforcement produced by electrical stimulation of septal area and other regions of rat brain. J Comp Physiol Psychol 47:419–427

Pellis SM, Pellis VC (2007) Rough-and-tumble play and the development of the social brain. Curr Dir Psychol Sci 16:95–98

Pereira ME, Fairbanks L (1993) Juvenile primates: life history, development and behavior. Oxford University Press, Oxford

Potegal M, Einon D (1989) Aggressive behaviors in adult rats deprived of playfighting experience as juveniles. Dev Psychobiol 22:159–172

Radoff J (2011) Game on: energize your business with social media games. Wiley, New York

Reiss S (2000) Who am I? The 16 basic desires that motivate our actions and define our personalities. Tarcher/Putnam, New York

Rilling J, Gutman D, Zeh T, Pagnoni G, Berns G, Kilts C (2002) A neural basis for social cooperation. Neuron 35:395–405

Rolls ET, O'Doherty J, Kringelbach ML, Francis S, Bowtell R, McGlone F (2003) Representations of pleasant and painful touch in the human orbitofrontal and cingulate cortices. Cereb Cortex 13:308–317

Russoniello CV, O'Brien K, Parks JM (2009) EEG, HRV and psychological correlates while playing Bejeweled II: a randomized controlled study. Stud Health Technol Inform 144:189–192

Ryan RM, Rigby CS, Przybylski A (2006) The motivational pull of video games: a self determination theory approach. Motiv Emot 30(4):347–364

Salen K, Zimmerman E (2004) Rules of play: game design fundamentals. MIT Press, Cambridge

Schmierbach M (2010) "Killing spree": exploring the connection between competitive game play and aggressive cognition. Commun Res 37:256–274

Seligman MEP (2011) Flourish: a visionary new understanding of happiness and well-being. Free Press, New York

Sharpe LL (2005a) Play fighting does not affect subsequent fighting success in wild meerkats. Anim Behav 69:1023–1029

Sharpe LL (2005b) Frequency of social play does not affect dispersal partnerships in wild meerkats. Anim Behav 70:559–569

Sharpe LL (2005c) Play does not enhance social cohesion in a cooperative mammal. Anim Behav 70:551–558

Sharpe LL, Cherry MI (2003) Social play does not reduce aggression in wild meerkats. Anim Behav 66:989–997

Staddon JE, Cerutti DT (2003) Operant conditioning. Annu Rev Psychol 54:115–144

Stetina BU, Kothgassner OD, Lehenbauer M, Kryspin-Exner I (2011) Beyond the fascination of online-games: probing addictive behavior and depression in the world of online-gaming. Comput Hum Behav 27:473–479

Suits B (1967) What is a game? Philos Sci 34:148–156

Wei HT, Chen MH, Huang PC, Bai YM (2012) The association between online gaming, social phobia, and depression: an internet survey. BMC Psychiatry 12:92

Part II
Player Behavior and Gameplay

Chapter 3
Pleasure in Pain: How Accumulation in Gaming Systems Can Lead to Grief

Selcen Ozturkcan and Sercan Sengun

Abstract This chapter applies the concepts of regulatory focus and regulatory fit into gaming structures and articulates their effects especially inside massively multiplayer games to understand the behavior of players inside gaming structures, as well as emotional transitions associated with them.

Keywords Regulatory focus • Regulatory fit • Games • Video games • Compulsory gaming

3.1 "Pleasure or Pain" Versus "Pleasure in Pain"

The scientific endeavor of pleasure and pain consists of a relatively established literature. Mercier (1901, p. 423) defines this long-standing contention between the opposing dichotomies as: "the integration or disintegration, the gain or loss [...] the success or failure [...] beneficial or harmful." Freud (2003), on the other hand, refers pleasure as a trade-off, where the individual is trying to balance the unpleasant tensions by avoiding them all together or producing pleasure.

Gaming or gamified systems are often associated with the frameworks of fun, joy, or amusement against any state of boredom, which are conceptually very similar to pleasure against pain. Additionally, the challenges and penalties involved as rewards are sometimes regarded as elements providing fun. Salen and Zimmerman (2004, p. 330) refer to these elements as "the carefully crafted arc of rewards and punishments that draws players into games and keep them playing [as well as that] connects pleasure to profitability." Indeed the concept of fun, as it's described under gaming or gamified systems, is truly a sensation that aligns with the pleasure in ordinary daily life. Some also refer it as the cognitive absorption experienced due to

S. Ozturkcan, Ph.D. (✉)
Associate Professor, Istanbul Bilgi University, Istanbul, Turkey
e-mail: selcen.ozturkcan@bilgi.edu.tr

S. Sengun, M.A.
Istanbul Bilgi University, Istanbul, Turkey
e-mail: sercan.sengun@bilgiedu.net

© Springer International Publishing Switzerland 2016
B. Bostan (ed.), *Gamer Psychology and Behavior*, International Series
on Computer Entertainment and Media Technology,
DOI 10.1007/978-3-319-29904-4_3

the concentration of playing, while some others refer it as the gratification pleasure that results from success upon winning (Wälder 1933). Lazzaro (2009) defines gaming fun as internal sensations, which occur while pursuing a goal and counts several different emotions that may be considered for having fun during a game play. These emotions range from surprise to naches/kvell (pride in something built, trained, created, etc.), from fiero (triumph over adversity) to schadenfreude (gloating over the misfortune of a rival).

It also seems possible to compensate the idea of fun inside gaming structures with the conditions of flow state. Flow state activities are distinguished by the intense challenge and skill combinations (Csikszentmihalyi 1997). Conditions of flow state include clear goals, immediate feedback, challenges that match skills, deep concentration, a feeling of control, the altered sense of time, and intrinsic rewards. Combined together, these create a flow state, which in turn transforms into a sensation that can also be deemed as fun.

In complementary studies, Bartle and Yee report different yet similar player types that enjoy various engagements in games. Bartle categorizes the players as Killers, Achievers, Socializers, and Explorers (Bartle n.d., 2004). Accordingly, killers want to be the strongest among players, while socializers want to bind with other players, explorers want to discover the virtual game world content, and lastly achievers want to finish (consume) the quests and goals within the game content. Yee reports similar game engagement reasons as creating relationships by interacting with other players, immersion by identifying with game content and experiencing the game world, and achievement by becoming powerful and beating the game content (Yee 2006).

Consequently, it is concluded that different player types demand different emotional approaches and leads within a given play (Ryan et al. 2006). Therefore, there is no one-size fits all formula regarding fun in games. Yet one thing seems conclusive; gaming fun is not just pure pleasure, but involves challenges, punishment, and hence even pain from time to time.

3.2 Prospect Theory: Foreseeing "Pleasure Versus Pain" as "Gain Versus Loss" in Decision Making

Prospect theory, a widely applied behavioral economic theory, describes choice-making behavior between probabilistic alternatives that involve risk with some known probabilistic outcomes (Kahneman and Tversky 1979). Accordingly, individuals' decisions are explained rather based on the expected potential value of losses and gains, but not the final outcome. Certain heuristics are used in individuals' evaluations of losses and gains to describe the real-life choices instead of often referred normative optimal decisions. The decision process of the prospect theory involves two stages, namely, editing and evaluation. First, a decision's expected outcomes are ordered. Here, individuals' considerations with regard to equivalent outcomes are set with regard to an identified reference point. Any outcome lesser than the reference is referred as "losses," while greater outcomes are referred as

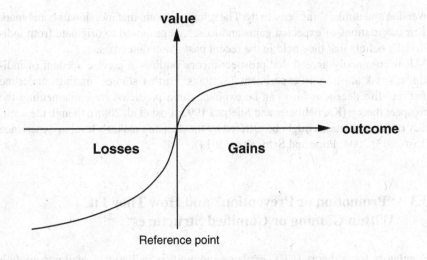

Fig. 3.1   Value function in prospect theory (Kahneman and Tversky 1979)

"gains" (Fig. 3.1). Alleviation of possible framing effects takes place during this stage, known as the editing stage (Tversky and Kahneman 1986). Next, an expected utility value is computed according to the potential outcomes and the related probabilities. Finally, the evaluation stage ends by choosing an alternative with the highest utility (Tversky and Kahneman 1981).

There are wide array of applications of the prospect theory. The fields of economics where prospect theory is most extensively applied are finance and insurance (Barberis 2013), which also led to the awarding of 2002 Nobel Prize in Economic Series to Daniel Kahneman. Some examples of the prospect theory's implementations in economics include the disposition effect, which explains investors' tendency to sell shares upon price increase, but keep assets upon value drop (Barberis and Xiong 2009). Similarly the reflection effect, which is reversing between risk preferences ranging from risk aversion to risk-seeking behavior in cases of gains or losses, provides another application (Kahneman and Tversky 1979). Another similar application is the pseudocertainty effect (Tversky and Kahneman 1986), which is also used to explain purchase decisions regarding insurance policies and/or lottery tickets. A further application is related with the mental accounting of individuals framing a potential outcome with regard to the utility they expect to receive in their minds (Kühberger et al. 1999). Following the widespread utilization in economics, other fields of research ranging from international relations, political science, and management to neuroscience have also utilized the prospect theory through various implementations (Levy 1992, 1997, 2003; Holmes et al. 2011; Boettcher 2004; D'Aveni 1989; Trepel et al. 2005) wherever risk is involved in decision making.

In a series of studies, Koszegi and Rabin (2006, 2007, 2009) examine individuals' considerations of gains and losses, to propose a framework applicable across disciplines. Accordingly, they define the difference between the consumption and expected consumption as the utility. The proposed utility function displays loss aversion and diminishing sensitivity. The reference point that individuals benchmark their calculations of expected gains and losses, is proposed to originate from individual's beliefs that they held in the recent past about outcomes.

It is commonly agreed that prospect theory outlines a precise account of individual's risk attitudes in experimental settings. Further studies' findings underline that real-life decisions also can be explained and predicted by implementing the prospect theory (Kachelmeier and Shehata 1992; Post et al. 2008), though the accuracy of the predictions might be differed by the decision maker's level of experience (List 2003, 2004; Pope and Schweitzer 2011).

3.3 "Promotion or Prevention" and How They Fit Within Gaming or Gamified Structures

Regulatory focus theory (RFT) explains and predicts individuals' goal pursuit with regard to their perceptions that take place during the decision-making process (Higgins 1997). Accordingly, there's a link between an individual's motivation and the way in which (s)he prefers to achieve his/her goals. The two possible self-regulatory orientations are (1) promotion and (2) prevention. The concerns of promotion and prevention focus differ. Promotion focus concentrates on advancement, growth, and accomplishment, while prevention focus concentrates on security, safety, and responsibility (Crowe and Higgins 1997).

Individual's involvement with a goal depends on the fit s/he perceives between the goal and his/her self-regulatory orientation. The higher the fit between an individual's goal orientation and the means of attaining that goal, the more engaged an individual becomes toward the task (Higgins et al. 2001; Higgins 2000, 2005). Regulatory fit strengthens positive responses toward more positive, negative responses toward more negative during valuation (Avnet and Higgins 2003; Higgins et al. 2003). Other studies have also reported similar intensifying effects of regulatory fit on persuasion (Cesario et al. 2008) and job satisfaction (Kruglanski et al. 2007).

An individual is inclined to maintain his/her personal values and beliefs while pursuing a specific goal, which is referred also as the regulatory orientation (Avnet and Higgins 2003). Individuals tend to welcome pleasure, but avoid pain with a regulatory focus. The concentration on the desired end states and the approach motivation to get to that state is the basic principle. Promotion focus concentrates on accomplishments, also referred to as gains. On the other hand, prevention-focus concentrates on safety and security, referred also as non-losses (Higgins et al. 2001). These different regulatory focuses influence the decision making process in terms of the preferred ways to achieve given goals (Halvorson and Higgins 2013). Individuals often regulate their goal-oriented behavior in distinct ways, either promotion focus orientation or prevention-focus orientation. Promotion focus orientation is concerned with aspirations and nurturance, and regulates behavior to maximize gains and minimize non-gains to reach a positive outcome. On the contrary, prevention-focus orientation regulates behavior with reference to negative

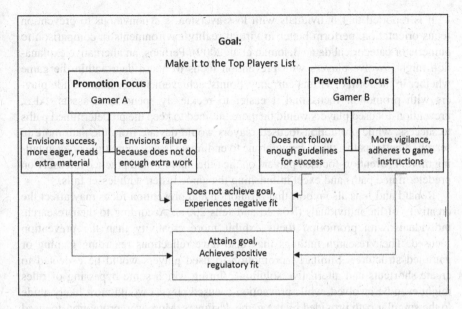

Fig. 3.2 Ways to achieve a goal for promotion and prevention focus gamers

outcomes in order to minimize losses and maximize non-losses (Higgins 1987; Markman and Brendl 2000).

An example might be useful to better depict the prospect theory and regulatory fit theory in understanding the gamer behavior. Figure 3.2 involves two gamers, A and B. They share a goal, which is to make it to the Top Players List. Gamer A is a promotion focus orientation individual. Gamer A perceives the goal as an ideal to satisfy his/her need for accomplishment. Gamer B is a prevention-focus orientation individual. The goal to make it to the Top Players List is something (s)he wants to fulfill because of his/her need for security, protection, and prevention of any nega-tive outcomes. Gamer A chooses an eager approach that includes reading extra materials, while Gamer B chooses a vigilant approach, where more careful attention is devoted to details and completion of all game elements.

It seems relatively plausible to reflect the prevention and promotion focus within the overall behaviors of game players. On the first level, it could be said that promotion-focused individuals would seemingly find it easier to participate in games with rewards while prevention-focused individuals would rather be con-cerned about gaming rules and guidelines. At the lack of written rules, prevention-focused gamers would rather observe other players for social cues rather than participation in the form of play. Once immersed with the rules of the game how-ever, they would adhere to guidelines set by the gaming community. Promotion-focused players, on the other hand, would be willing to benefit from external resources and hence they'd be rather experimental. Prevention-focused players would be rather risk-averse, and focus solely on success via known rules, and there-fore less inclined to experimentation.

It is reported that individuals with loss aversion, a synonymous to prevention focus orientation, perform better in virtual reality environments in comparison to numeric or categorical data (Bateman et al. 2009). Perhaps, an alternative explanation might involve players with prevention focus to hoard data within the game whether in the form of virtual currency, points, achievements, or items, while players with promotion focus find it easier to recklessly spend such assets. Also, prevention-focused players would be more inclined to keep the predetermined paths to success, while promotion-focused players would deviate from the path more in search of better paths, while being prone to ending up losing more time or even failing more. Prevention-focused players on the other hand would practice intensely on predetermined paths and excel in finishing the game faster, with lesser fails.

Ronald and Jens also report that promotion and prevention focus may affect the creativity of the individuals (Ronald and Jens 2001). According to their research, individuals with promotion focus exhibit more creativity than the prevention focused. Their research findings may also have reflections regarding gaming or gamified structures. Similarly, promotion-focused players would be expected to create shortcuts and alternative solutions, during which some bypassing of rules might even be involved, while prevention-focused players would most likely abide to the singular path provided by the game designers. Moreover, promotion-focused players may find it easier to convert games into expression tools in ways not primarily intended by their producers. For example, inside Rockstar Games' 2013-released game Grand Theft Auto V, a player is reported to start a blog that consisted solely of screenshots of a game character lifting random things with his forklift (Ashcraft 2013). Instead of pursuing the usual criteria of success via beating quests or advancing the narrative, this player seems to have converted the game into a different creative outlet. In this light, the overall approach in prevention or promotion focus may indicate differences in game choices too; promotion-focused players may feel comfortable in playing more open-world and endless games, while prevention-focused players would rather choose games with singular or limited flows where an ending, or at least a closure, is possible.

The regulatory focus might also explain some gaming-related addiction issues. Previously the effects of regulatory focus were researched in the domain of self-regulation in relation to consumer psychology and goal orientation (Freitas et al. 2002; Higgins 2002). It had been suggested that prevention-focused individuals fare better under conditions where they had to resist temptation. According to a research on the effects of addiction prevention messages inside games, it was found that negative messages are significantly effective for promotion focused players while positive messages influence prevention focused players significantly (Ho et al. 2011).

The concept of regulatory focus was later expanded into the concept of regulatory fit. Freitas and Higgins propose that not only individuals but also actions could have an innate emphasis on a certain regulatory focus. Thus, when the focus of the action at hand and the individual who performs it match, this creates a situation called the regulatory fit (Freitas and Higgins 2002). Adapting this into a gaming or gamified system, it could be said that gaining something for seemingly free or little effort inside the system (watch this ad video and earn 100 gold) is indeed a rather promotion-focused action, while the prospect of loss (finish this action in next 5 min or you lose 100 gold) creates a prevention-focused action. While testing regulatory fit with awarding and punishing conditions, Spiegel et al. proposed that promotion-focused individuals perform better under awarding systems as opposed to prevention focused individuals performing better under punishing conditions (Spiegel et al. 2004). These findings require further testing and explanation regarding the games and gaming systems. For instance, it could be proposed that promotion-focused players would find easier and more rewarding games way more engaging than harder games that involve punishments (and vice versa for prevention focused players). These conclusions do not contradict with previous proposals in which promotion-focused players found it easier to get into (decide to play) games and were distracted easily during the course of play from the linear paths of success— yet their combination form curious implications. It has already been suggested that prevention-focused players make slower game selecting decisions, would rather focus on game models that have definitive progress and preferably conditions for an ending, experiment less, fail less and succeed more in numerical and categorical terms. The previously mentioned study also implies that, they would seemingly expect less awarding and more punishing gaming systems. This could be initially accepted as an abnormal gaming behavior—since prevention focused players would be more focused on success, should they not have fared better under more rewarding approaches? However, this phenomenon could be analyzed under the conditions that a player decides to stop playing a game and moves onto another one. Promotion-focused players may find it easier to get into games, experiment, and deviate, yet they seemingly also find it easier to leave a game too. This makes it more feasible for them to gather as much reward in the shortest time possible since they could move on anytime without focusing on or fulfilling the final success criteria of the game. Prevention-focused players would rather stay in the game till they achieve the predetermined success criteria, thus rewards along the way are less interesting to them. They would rather face challenges along the way to achieving the final closure.

However, some of these proposals were tackled by us in a recent research where findings indicated punishing systems resulting in higher engagement from both groups (Öztürkcan and Şengün 2015). These findings highlighted some bullet points for the domain of game design in concluding that the dichotomy of punishing vs. awarding systems (as described by Spiegel et al.) not performing to expectations in games. The correct dichotomy for game systems was indeed punishing versus less punishing systems. Both approaches had to inherit some awards; however the true engagement was a result of refraining from punishments.

3.4 Regulatory Focus, Regulatory Fit, and Abnormal Gaming Behavior

Several propositions emerge upon application of the regulatory fit theory to the gaming or gamified systems. Gaming or gamified systems are rather inherently promotion focused, highlighting participation and accomplishments. However, they could hardly be designed for endless winning and providing endless content as a result. Instead, they employ methods for diminishing the accumulated resources, which in turn triggers actions with regard to the prevention focus. When participants who have entered the system expecting promotion focus (or vice versa) start to feel the presence of prevention focus (or vice versa), the regulatory fit begins to get damaged or loosen. When there is lack of fit, some participants feel left out and loose motivation. Moreover, in the cases of resuming back the fit, some abnormal behaviors may occur. To continue from the previous examples, prevention-focused players find it harder to get into a game and when they do, instead of experimenting and deviating, they prefer fulfilling the pre-determined success criteria. Hence, they do not often feel a regulatory fit with the game initially as most games employ a learning curve that aims to teach them how to play. These beginning sections are inherently promotion focused and "[viewed] as a price of admission to what is hoped will be future fulfilling game experiences" (Przybylski et al. 2010, p. 156). The ending of the game is still very far away and in most of the cases the game does not have full options available, thus presenting little challenge. As the game progresses, playing it transforms into a more prevention-focused action. The challenge is heightened, the game requires more time investment, and there has been an accumulation of digital data or assets valid to the gaming system. The prevention-focused player, who lacked a regulatory fit at the promotion-focused on the beginning of the game, is reconnected to the system, which now became more prevention focused. In contrast to a promotion-focused player, the prevention-focused player would find it harder to abandon a game as (s)he progresses deeper into it. On the other hand, the promotion-focused player begins the game with a regulatory fit. As the game progresses, the focus transforms into a preventive one, causing a fracture in the regulatory fit. Instead of conforming to the system of challenges and punishments, promotion-focused player would most likely look for ways to deviate from the game play and if none are present, would be inclined to move onto another game.

The remaining parts of this study would like to discuss the effects of regulatory focus and regulatory fit within a certain game genre (massively multiplayer role playing games) and especially within a selected game from this genre (World of Warcraft). Massively multiplayer online games seem ideal for this purpose for several reasons. First of all, these games employ powerful accumulation schemes be it social connections, enduring characters or account-bound achievements, items and cosmetic adjustments. They also employ punishments within these accumulation schemes, such as time-limited achievements or items, which make transformation of regulatory focus possible. Secondly, these games are well documented in academic research in terms of player engagement, social relations, and abnormal behaviors, such as addiction. And last of all, massively multiplayer online games have different connotations regarding finishing the game or stopping to play—more specifically, a massively multiplayer online game such as World of Warcraft "never truly ends" (Boyns et al. 2009).

In massively multiplayer online gaming, players invest long hours into accumulating resources inside the gaming system. Most of these resources are only accessible as long as the game account is active and the level of their worth can only be kept stable by active participation in the game—usually in long play hours. Various studies confirm that in the later stages of these games, players show addictive or compulsive behaviors to protect their investments (Wan and Chiou 2006a, b; Rooji et al. 2009; Lu and Wang 2008; Collins et al. 2012; Liu and Peng 2009; Peter and Malesky 2008). This is seemingly a reconnection with prevention focus. In the later stages of these types of games, promotion-focused players would find it easier to change games while prevention-focused players would most likely choose to stay. In contrast, in the earlier stage of these games, promotion-focused players will succeed less and slower since they would be more willing to spend their money, equipment, or resources quickly and the game would be willing to help and provide them easy success.

Like in many other massively multiplayer online role playing games, in World of Warcraft, these resources include social connections, characters, achievements, items, pets, mounts, and other cosmetic alterations. In 2012, World of Warcraft has stripped many achievements, pets, and mounts from being bound to in-game characters and made them bound to the player's account, a decision which technically binds them to the players themselves (Torres 2012). As much as earning many of these assets were promotion-focused actions themselves, maintaining them becomes a prevention-focused action in the long run.

One of the less obscure resources to apply regulatory focus behaviors inside World of Warcraft would be social capital. As described by Coleman, social capital refers to resources accumulated within social networks (Coleman 1998). There are different views on the relationship between social capital and media. While some studies propose that media consumption might be inversely related to the levels of social capital (Putnam 2001), others suggest that richer media environments may lead to stronger connections and more social capital (Kiesler and Sproull 1992; Haythornthwaite 2002). To explain social capital inside World of Warcraft better, Guo and Barnes formed a research construct called perceived social status which explains the influence of player's position inside the game and resulted in "forming a strong desire toward acquiring advanced, valuable virtual items" (Guo and Barnes 2012). Although Taylor proposes that presence in the out of game forum or guild boards are primary social capital resource for massively multiplayer online games (Taylor 2009), Guo & Barnes' findings propose that social capital inside World of Warcraft is primarily formed by the accumulation of virtual items and upkeeps in the same way. A previous study investigates social behavior within World of Warcraft in terms of introvertedness and extrovertedness (Yee et al. 2011). It concludes that extroverts change guilds more often and prefer group activities while introverts prefer solo activities and are more likely to have vanity items. The relationship between introvertedness/extrovertedness and regulatory focus (obtaining a positive outcome vs. avoiding a negative outcome) was also previously tested (Bai et al. 2009). In the light of the data, the players who change guilds more often and prefer group activities could be associated with promotion focus and the players who prefer solo activities could be associated with prevention focus. However, when a prevention-focused player (although primarily preferring solo play) ultimately gets into a guild, the regulatory fit is transformed into earning and upkeeping social capital. The prevention-focused players would find it harder to leave guilds once they are inside. Some previous studies show that players who are in a guild, and therefore have probably accumulated some social capital within it, spend more time online than players who are not (Ducheneaut et al. 2006; Seay et al. 2004). A nationwide study in Germany proposes that online games such as strategy and shooters contribute less to video game dependency than massively multiplayer online role playing games (Rehbein et al. 2010). The complex social structures of massively multiplayer online role playing games coupled with prevention-focused behaviors may be the key to explaining these dependencies.

Another aspect of the regulatory focus is hoarding other resources in massively multiplayer games. Achievements and vanity (cosmetic) items are among the most effective of these resources. According to studies in World of Warcraft, "achievement oriented players reported a higher weekly play time and a lower stop rate" (Debeauvais et al. 2011). These players are seemingly correlated with prevention-focused players who have ventured deeper into the game and accepted achievements as the predetermined success points in this never ending game. Promotion-focused players would probably less care about finishing as much achievement as possible or would feel less discomfort in missing an achievement. Another study proposed that achievement-oriented motivations were negatively related to positive personality traits such as conscientiousness, agreeableness and openness yet were positively related to traits such as neuroticism (Graham and Gosling 2013). This seemingly pushes achievement-seeking behavior into the realm of abnormal gaming behavior, resulting from a negative transformation of regulatory fit.

As much as achievement hoarding, item hoarding is also a prediction for prevention focus. In a March 2015 article, massively multiplayer online gaming community Massively Overpowered asks its readers what kind of mistakes they make in massively multiplayer online games (Lefebvre 2015). Among the replies left as comments to the page some resonate in this issue. User wild_abyss quotes: "you hoard all your potions 'in case I need them later' and then never end up using them." Another user Mansemat quotes: "I won't use items like potions and scrolls. I'll just horde them [...] Also, if it's a cosmetic item that has a finite duration, I'll never use it. I'll just throw it in the bank." The behavior defined by these users is prevention focused. Promotion-focused players on the other hand would find it much easier to spend limited items such as potions, money, etc. for instant results instead of waiting for the perfect time to use them.

A final study found a relation between regulatory focus and perfectionism (Mautz 2013). The study concludes that promotion focus was a prediction for high standards and prevention focus was a prediction for self-evaluative perfectionism. This is relevant to massively multiplayer online games like World of Warcraft, since they present their players with a large number of multifaceted, long-term achievements. An achievement in World of Warcraft is called What a Long, Strange Trip It's Been, and it requires the players to complete timed holiday sub-achievements that become available around the year. If a player misses a holiday achievement during that holiday, the player will need to wait for the next year's holiday to complete it. While promotion-focused players would seemingly be more interested in trying to pursue this achievement, they would not feel a discomfort in not finalizing it. Prevention-focused players on the other hand would be less inclined to decide to pursue this achievement, yet once they do they would want to see it to the end. About a similar scenario, a World of Warcraft blogger reads: "I remember looking [at this achievement] back in 2010 and thinking this was something I would never do" (Zielenkievicz 2013); however, once set out to it, the blogger pursues the achievement for 2 years—after which he finally gains it.

3.5   Conclusion

This study aimed to apply the concepts of regulatory focus and regulatory fit inside gaming structures. Prospect theory and regulatory fit theory were used in explaining complex issues in decision making, motivation, inspiration, goal attainment, and self-construction. To the best of our knowledge, this study is a pioneer in using this framework in explaining and predicting player behavior.

The dichotomy of prevention versus promotion-focused behaviors could easily be observed in games. This study focused on studies made around World of Warcraft, a massively multiplayer online role playing game, to find out and elucidate their relation with regulatory focus and regulatory fit.

It was proposed that on the one hand promotion-focused players would find it easier to get into any game. They would be inclined to take more risks during play, thus dying or failing more. Promotion-focused players could pursue the success criteria of the game at hand as well as deviating from them to have more experimental play. It would be unsurprising to find a promotion-focused player while using a game in ways unintended or unseen by its creators. Prevention-focused players on the other hand would find it harder to get into game. They would avoid risks, experiment less and as a result die or fail less. Prevention-focused players would focus on the ultimate success criteria of the game and would be less likely to deviate from its path. In numerical or categorical data, prevention-focused players would seem to be more successful than promotion-focused players since they would be more goal oriented. When it comes to leaving a game though, promotion-focused players would find it easier to stop playing a game while a prevention-focused player would find it harder to leave the accumulated resources inside the game, causing abnormal gaming behaviors that tether on the brink of addiction.

In a massively multiplayer online game, such as World of Warcraft, promotion focused players would find it easier to spend resources for instantaneous advantages (while prevention-focused players would hoard them in waiting for the best time to use them), would be more interested in pursuing achievements but less interested in finalizing them (while prevention-focused players would be less interested in pursuing achievements but more obsessed in finalizing them once they do) and have different behavior approaches for social capital. Promotion focused players would find it easier to surf through player guilds and get groups while prevention-focused players would rather play solo. However, once they find themselves inside a guild, prevention focused players would be highly sensitive about maintaining their social status within it, resulting in longer play hours.

This study aimed to explain the effects of regulatory focus and regulatory fit inside games in a broad approach. Further studies examining these effects in narrower issues in gaming are seemingly needed and could prove potential for further research.

References

Ashcraft B (2013) GTA V's Trevor sure likes forklifting some weird things. 17 October 2013. Kotaku. http://kotaku.com/trevor-from-gta-v-makes-fascinating-internet-fodder-1446915540. Accessed 27 Sept 2015

Avnet T, Higgins ET (2003) Locomotion, assessment, and regulatory fit: value transfer from how to what. J Exp Soc Psychol 39:525–530

Bai XJ, Zhu ZH, Shen DL, Liu N (2009) Autonomic nervous arousal and behavioral response of punishment and rewards in extroverts and introverts. Acta Psychol Sin 6

Barberis NC (2013) Thirty years of prospect in economics: a review and assessment. J Econ Perspect 27:173–196

Barberis NC, Xiong W (2009) What drives the disposition effect? An analysis of a long-standing preference-based explanation. J Financ 64:751–784

Bartle RA (2004) Designing virtual worlds. New Riders, San Francisco

Bartle RA (n.d.) Hearts, clubs, diamonds, spades: players who suit MUDs. http://mud.co.uk/richard/hcds.htm. Accessed 24 Sept 2015

Bateman IJ, Day BH, Jones AP, Jude S (2009) Reducing gain–loss asymmetry: a virtual reality choice experiment valuing land use change. J Environ Econ Manag 58(1):106–118

Boettcher WA (2004) The prospects for prospect theory: an empirical evaluation of international relations applications of framing and loss aversion. Polit Psychol 25:331–362

Boyns D, Forghani S, Sosnovskaya E (2009) MMORPG worlds: on the construction of social reality in World of Warcraft. In: Heider D (ed) Living virtually: researching new worlds. Peter Lang, New York, pp 67–92

Cesario J, Higgins ET, Scholer AA (2008) Regulatory fit and persuasion: basic principles and remaining questions. Soc Personal Psychol Compass 2:444–463

Coleman JS (1998) Social capital in the creation of human capital. Am J Sociol 94:95–120

Collins E, Freeman J, Chamarro-Premuzic T (2012) Personality traits associated with problematic and non-problematic massively multiplayer online role playing game use. Personal Individ Differ 52(2):133–138

Crowe E, Higgins ET (1997) Regulatory focus and strategic inclinations: promotion and prevention in decision-making. Organ Behav Hum Decis Process 69:117–132

Csikszentmihalyi M (1997) Finding flow. Basic Books, New York

D'Aveni RA (1989) Dependability and organizational bankruptcy: an application of agency and prospect theory. Manag Sci 35:1120–1138

Debeauvais T, Nardi B, Schiano DJ, Ducheneaut N, Yee N (2011) If you build it they might stay: retention mechanisms in World of Warcraft. In: Cavazza M, Isbister K, Rich C (eds) FDG '11 proceedings of the 6th international conference on foundations of digital games. ACM, New York, pp 180–187

Ducheneaut N, Yee N, Nickell E, Moore RJ (2006) Alone together? Exploring the social dynamics of massively multiplayer online games. In: Grinter R, Rodden T, Aoki P, Cutrell E, Jeffries R,

Olson G (eds) Proceedings of ACM CHI 2006 conference on human factors in computing systems. ACM, Montreal, pp 407–416

Freitas AL, Higgins ET (2002) Enjoying goal-directed action: the role of regulatory fit. Psychol Sci 13(1):1–6

Freitas AL, Liberman N, Higgins ET (2002) Regulatory fit and resisting temptation during goal pursuit. J Exp Soc Psychol 38(3):291–298

Freud S (2003) Beyond the pleasure principle and other writings (trans: Reddick J). Penguin Books, London

Graham LT, Gosling SD (2013) Personality profiles associated with different motivations for playing World of Warcraft. Cyberpsychol Behav Soc Netw 16(3):189–193

Guo Y, Barnes SJ (2012) Explaining purchasing behaviour within World of Warcraft. J Comp Inform Syst 52(3):18–30

Halvorson HG, Higgins ET (2013) Do you play to win—or to not lose? March 2013. Harvard Business Review. https://hbr.org/2013/03/do-you-play-to-win-or-to-not-lose? Accessed 27 Sept 2015

Haythornthwaite C (2002) Strong, weak, and latent ties and the impact of new media. Inform Soc 18:385–401

Higgins ET (1987) Self-discrepancy: a theory relating self and affect. Psychol Rev 94:319–340

Higgins ET (1997) Beyond pleasure and pain. Am Psychol 52:1280–1300

Higgins ET (2000) Making a good decision: value from fit. Am Psychol 55:1217–1230

Higgins ET (2002) How self-regulation creates distinct values: the case of promotion and prevention decision making. J Consum Psychol 12(3):177–191

Higgins ET (2005) Value from regulatory fit. Curr Dir Psychol Sci 14:209–213

Higgins ET, Friedman RS, Harlow RE, Idson LC, Ayduk ON, Taylor A (2001) Achievement orientations from subjective histories of success: promotion pride versus prevention pride. Eur J Soc Psychol 31:3–23

Higgins JPT, Thompson SG, Deeks JJ, Altman DG (2003) Measuring inconsistency in meta-analyses. BMJ 327:557–560

Ho S, Putthiwanit C, Chia-Ying L (2011) May I continue or should I stop? The effects of regulatory focus and message framings on video game players' self-control. Int J Bus Soc Sci 2(12):194–200

Holmes RM, Bromiley P, Devers CE, Holcomb TR, McGuire JB (2011) Management theory applications of prospect theory: accomplishments, challenges, and opportunities. J Manag 37:1069–1107

Kachelmeier S, Shehata M (1992) Examining risk preferences under high monetary incentives: experimental evidence from the People's Republic of China. Am Econ Rev 82:1120–1141

Kahneman D, Tversky A (1979) Prospect theory: an analysis of decision under risk. Econometrica 47:263–291

Kiesler S, Sproull L (1992) Group decision making and communication technology. Org Behav Human Decis Proc 52(1):96–123

Koszegi B, Rabin M (2006) A model of reference-dependent preferences. Q J Econ 47:263–291

Koszegi B, Rabin M (2007) Reference-dependent risk attitudes. Am Econ Rev 97:1047–1073

Koszegi B, Rabin M (2009) Reference-dependent consumption plans. Am Econ Rev 99:909–936

Kruglanski AW, Pierro A, Higgins ET, Capozza D (2007) On the move or staying put: locomotion, need for closure, and reactions to organizational change. J Appl Soc Psychol 37:1305–1340

Kühberger A, Schulte-Mecklenbeck M, Perner J (1999) The effects of framing, reflection, probability and payoff on risk preference in choice tasks. Organ Behav Hum Decis Process 78:204–231

Lazzaro N (2009) Understand emotions. In: Bateman C, Bartle R (eds) Beyond game design: nine steps towards creating better videogames. Cengage Learning, Hampshire, pp 3–47

Lefebvre E (2015) The daily grind: what stupid mistake do you keep making in an MMO? 30 March 2015. Massively Overpowered. http://massivelyop.com/2015/03/30/the-daily-grind-what-stupid-mistake-do-you-keep-making-in-an-mmo/. Accessed 27 Sept 2015

Levy JS (1992) Prospect theory and international relations: theoretical applications and analytical problems. Polit Psychol 13:283–310

Levy JS (1997) Prospect theory, rational choice, and international relations. Int Stud Q 41: 87–112

Levy JS (2003) Applications of prospect theory to political science. Synthese 135:215–241

List J (2003) Does market experience eliminate market anomalies? Quart J Econ Perspect 118:41–71

List J (2004) Neoclassical theory versus prospect theory: evidence from the marketplace. Econometrica 72:615–625

Liu M, Peng W (2009) Cognitive and psychological predictors of the negative outcomes associated with playing MMOGs (massively multiplayer online games). Comput Hum Behav 25(6):1306–1311

Lu H, Wang S (2008) The role of internet addiction in online game royalty: an exploratory study. Internet Res 18(5):499–519

Markman AB, Brendl M (2000) The influence of goals on value and choice. Psychol Learn Motiv 39:97–128

Mautz CP (2013) Reinforcement sensitivity and regulatory focus predict perfectionism. MA thesis, Appalachian State University

Mercier CA (1901) Psychology: normal and morbid. Swan Sonnenschein, New York

Öztürkcan S, Şengün S (2015) Gaining rewards vs avoiding loss: when does gamification stop being fun? In: Davis D, Gangadharbatla H (eds) Handbook of research on trends in gamification. IGI Global, Hershey, pp 48–71

Peter CS, Malesky LA (2008) Problematic usage among highly-engaged players of massively multiplayer online role playing games. Cyberpsychol Behav 11(4):481–484

Pope D, Schweitzer M (2011) Is Tiger Woods loss averse? Persistent bias in the face of experience, competition, and high stakes. Am Econ Rev 101:129–157

Post T, Assem MVD, Baltussen G, Thaler R (2008) Deal or no deal? Decision-making under risk in a large-payoff game show. Am Econ Rev 98:38–71

Przybylski AK, Rigby CS, Ryan RM (2010) A motivational model of video game engagement. Rev Gen Psychol 13(2):154–166

Putnam RD (2001) Social capital: measurement and consequences. Isuma: Can J Policy Res 2(Spring):41–51

Rehbein F, Kleimann M, Mößle T (2010) Prevalence and risk factors of video game dependency in adolescence: results of a German nationwide survey. Cyberpsychol Behav Soc Netw 13(3):269–277

Ronald F, Jens F (2001) The effects of promotion and prevention cues on creativity. J Pers Soc Psychol 81(6):1001–1013

Rooji AJ, Schoenmakers TM, Eijnden RJJM, Mheen D (2009) Compulsive internet use: the role of online gaming and other internet applications. J Adolesc Health 47(1):51–57

Ryan RM, Rigby CS, Przybylski AK (2006) Motivational pull of video games: a self-determination theory approach. Motiv Emot 30:347–365

Salen K, Zimmerman E (2004) Rules of play: game design fundamentals. MIT, Cambridge

Seay AF, Jerome WJ, Lee KS, Kraut RE (2004) Project massive: a study of online gaming communities. In: Dykstra-Erickson E, Tscheligi M (eds) Proceedings of CHI '04 extended abstracts on human factors in computing systems. ACM, New York, pp 1421–1424

Spiegel S, Grant-Pillow H, Higgins ET (2004) How regulatory fit enhances motivational strength during goal pursuit. Eur J Soc Psychol 34(1):39–54

Taylor TL (2009) Play between worlds: exploring online game culture. MIT, Cambridge

Torres R (2012) What you should know about account-wide pets, mounts and achievements, 28 August 2012. Engadget. http://www.engadget.com/2012/08/28/what-you-should-know-about-account-wide-pets-mounts-and-achieve/. Accessed 27 Sept 2015

Trepel C, Fox CR, Poldrack RA (2005) Prospect theory on the brain? Toward a cognitive neuroscience of decision under risk. Cogn Brain Res 23:34–50

Tversky A, Kahneman D (1981) The framing of decisions and the psychology of choice. Science 211:453–458

Tversky A, Kahneman D (1986) Rational choice and the framing of decisions. J Bus 59:251–278

Wälder R (1933) The psychoanalytic theory of play. Psychoanal Quart 2:208–224

Wan C, Chiou W (2006a) Why are adolescents addicted to online gaming? An interview study in Taiwan. Cyberpsychol Behav 9(6):762–766

Wan C, Chiou W (2006b) Psychological motives and online games addiction: a test of flow theory and humanistic needs theory for Taiwanese adolescents. Cyberpsychol Behav 9(3):317–324

Yee N (2006) The psychology of MMORPGs: emotional investment, motivations, relationship formation, and problematic usage. In: Schroeder R, Axelsson A (eds) Avatars at work and play: collaboration and interaction in shared virtual environments. Springer, London, pp 187–207

Yee N, Ducheneaut N, Nelson L, Likarish P (2011) Introverted elves & conscientious gnomes: the expression of personality in World of Warcraft. In: Tan D, Fitzpatrick G, Gutwin C, Begole B, Kellogg WA (eds) CHI '11 proceedings of the SIGCHI conference on human factors in computing systems. ACM, New York, pp 753–762

Zielenkievicz, N (2013) WoW! Thoughts!—on what a long, strange trip it's been. 31 October 2013. Mash Those Buttons. http://mashthosebuttons.com/2013/10/wow-thoughts-on-what-a--long-strange-trip-its-been/. Accessed 27 Sept 2015

Chapter 4
Goal-Directed Player Behavior in Computer Games

Barbaros Bostan and Sercan Altun

Abstract This study applies a motivated action model to analyze the basics of goal-directed player behavior in computer games and uses a motivational framework to investigate the relation of various gaming situations with different player needs. The game selected for this study is an action-adventure game named *Middle-earth: Shadows of Mordor*. The first section attempts to find the relationship between psychological needs and game mechanics, showing that the restrictions imposed by the game mechanics significantly reduce the number of player needs satisfied by a game. The second section investigates the anatomy of choices made by players in different gaming situations. Each gaming situation from *Shadows of Mordor* is described with appropriate incentives, goals, motivations, actions, reinforcers, and punishers.

Keywords Player psychology • Player behavior • Goal-directed behavior • Player motivations

4.1 Introduction

Human behavior is geared to effecting change in the environment, and changes in the environment are possible through the attainment of goals or disengagement from unattainable goals, which are facilitated by coordination of perceptions, skills, activities, and emotions (Heckhausen and Heckhausen 2005). Motivation to reach a goal is influenced by both personal and situational factors. Personal factors are a person's needs, motives, and goals and situational factors are opportunities and possible incentives provided by the environment. According to Murray (1938), goal-directed human behavior can be explained by continuous interactions between

B. Bostan, Ph.D. (✉)
Department of Information Systems and Technologies, Yeditepe University, Istanbul, Turkey
e-mail: bbostan@yeditepe.edu.tr

S. Altun, B.S.
Department of Game Design, Bahçeşehir University, Istanbul, Turkey
e-mail: altun.sercan@gmail.com

© Springer International Publishing Switzerland 2016
B. Bostan (ed.), *Gamer Psychology and Behavior*, International Series
on Computer Entertainment and Media Technology,
DOI 10.1007/978-3-319-29904-4_4

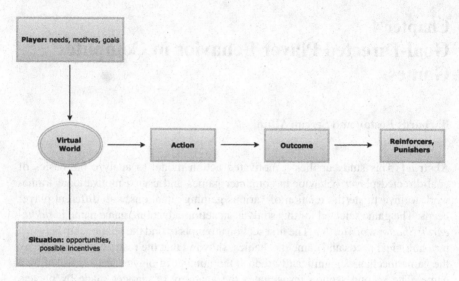

Fig. 4.1 A modified version of the motivated action model (Heckhausen and Heckhausen 2005)

individuals and their environments. Interactions between personal and situational factors trigger actions. Outcomes are the results of actions, and reinforcers/punishers are consequences that arise from outcomes. This basic structure of human behavior is also applicable to game players who experience different gaming situations with different incentives within a virtual world and then decide on an action based on their motives, needs, and goals. Fig 4.1 shows the motivated action model for game players.

Reinforcers are stimuli that select appropriate behaviors and teach us what to do; punishers are stimuli that select against appropriate behaviors and teach us what not to do (Skinner 1938, 1953; Staddon and Simmelhag 1971). Incentives are external stimuli that motivate or induce behavior (Bolles 1975; Logan and Wagner 1965). A positive incentive motivates behavior and a negative incentive motivates avoidance behavior. Briefly, reinforcers and punishers are the actual consequences of behavior, whereas positive and negative incentives are the anticipated consequences. The association between the reinforcers/punishers and incentives may also end up as generalizations. If a response consistently results in a reinforcer/punisher, then that reinforcer/punisher might become a positive/negative incentive (Bolles 1975; Logan 1960). Reinforcers and punishers also provide a feedback mechanism for goal-directed behavior. Feedback tells people how they are progressing relative to a goal; and goals do not motivate behavior unless feedback is provided (Bandura and Cervone 1983).

Gamer behavior will be analyzed according to the motivated action model described above but the motivational analysis in this chapter uses psychological needs. A need refers to a potentiality or readiness to respond in a certain way under given conditions and each need is characterized by a certain effect or the occurrence of a certain trend (Murray 1938). The most popular study on human needs is conducted by Maslow (1943, 1968) who identifies a hierarchy of needs in man ranging from the lower-order physiological drives to higher-order psychological motivations. McDougall (1908) made the pioneering attempt to define the whole human behavior in terms of innate psychophysical dispositions (instincts), but it was Murray (1938) who formalized the study of needs. His 3-year study at the Harvard Psychological Clinic was conducted by 28 psychologists of various schools, among whom were three physicians and five psychoanalysts. The psychogenic needs of Murray, which are psychological in nature, are not static entities but the result of both internal and external forces, and are concerned with mental and emotional states of a person. Twenty-seven psychogenic needs of this framework have already been analyzed by Bostan (2009) in relation to the gaming situations of a RPG. This chapter attempts to take this study one step further by analyzing the common fusions of individual needs and by defining the driving game mechanics behind them, also analyzing various gaming situations to understand the basics of gamer behavior. The needs investigated are given below with related actions for each one of them (Table 4.1).

4.2 Game Mechanics

The needs framework of Murray (1938) can theoretically be applied to computer game of any genre, but the range of needs satisfied by a computer game is usually limited by its content and rules of play. For example, information needs are prominent in adventure games where players focus on exploration and puzzle-solving within a narrative framework, whereas social simulation games, such as The Sims, are built on the theme of affiliation. In this regard, role-playing games are perfect candidates for analyzing the motivational aspects of a gaming experience because they satisfy a wider range of psychological needs. But since role-playing games are analyzed within this motivational framework before, we choose an action-adventure game this time for this chapter.

The game selected for this study is Shadows of Mordor developed by Monolith Productions and published by Warner Bros. The game was released for Microsoft Windows, PlayStation 4, and Xbox One in September 2014 and released for PlayStation 3 and Xbox 360 in November 2014. It won the "Game of the Year" award from GameSpot (2014) and Game Developer's Choice Awards (2015). The story of the game takes place between the events of The Hobbit and The Lord of the Rings. The players control Talion, a ranger who was killed by the Black Hand of Sauron. Talion's spirit merged with the wraith of the Elf Lord Celebrimbor, and together they try to avenge the death of their loved ones. Players can engage in melee combat and utilize some of the wraith abilities to fight against enemies. The game uses the Nemesis System, an intriguing hierarchy of enemies that gives every victory and defeat extra meaning. The player can upgrade his/her weapons with runes acquired from killed enemies and it is also possible to brand or control enemies so that the player can use them as allies in combat or assassins in the Uruk hierarchy.

Table 4.1 Needs and actions related with them

Need	Related actions
Acquisition (nAcq)	To gain possessions and property. To grasp, snatch or steal things. To bargain or gamble. To work for money or goods
Construction (nCons)	To create and build new objects/items. To combine and configure objects
Order (nOrd)	To arrange, organize, put away objects. To be tidy and clean
Retention (nRet)	To retain possession of things. To refuse to give or lend. To hoard. To be frugal, economical, and miserly
Aggression (nAgg)	To assault or injure a person. To murder. To belittle, harm, blame, accuse, or maliciously ridicule a person
Blamavoidance (nBlam)	To avoid blame or punishment. To be well behaved and obey the law. To be concerned about public opinion
Counteraction (nCnt)	To overcome defeat by restriving and retaliating. To defend one's honor in action
Defendance (nDfd)	To defend oneself against criticism or blame. To conceal or justify a misdeed, failure, or humiliation. To offer extenuations, explanations, and excuses
Deference (nDef)	To admire and willingly follow a superior allied person. To co-operate with a leader. To serve gladly
Dominance (nDom)	To influence or control others. To persuade, prohibit, dictate. To lead and direct. To restrain. To organize the behavior of a group
Abasement (nAba)	To surrender. To comply and accept punishment. To apologize, confess, atone. To admit inferiority, error, wrongdoing, or defeat
Affiliation (nAff)	To form friendships and associations. To greet, join, and live with others. To co-operate and converse sociably with others. To join groups
Nurturance (nNur)	To nourish, aid, or protect a helpless person. To express sympathy. To have a child
Rejection (nRej)	To snub, ignore, or exclude a person. To remain aloof and indifferent. To be discriminating. To exclude, abandon, expel, or remain indifferent to an inferior
Succorance (nSuc)	To seek aid, protection, or sympathy. To cry for help. To plead for mercy. To be dependent
Achievement (nAch)	To overcome obstacles, to exercise power, to strive to do something difficult as well and as quickly as possible. To excel one's self. To rival and surpass others
Autonomy (nAuto)	To resist influence or coercion. To defy an authority or seek freedom. To strive for independence
Harmavoidance (nHarm)	To avoid pain, physical injury, illness, and death. To escape from a dangerous situation. To take precautionary measures
Infavoidance (nInf)	To avoid failure, shame, humiliation, ridicule. To refrain from attempting to do something that is beyond one's powers. To conceal a disfigurement
Recognition (nRec)	To excite praise and commendation. To demand respect. To boast and exhibit one's accomplishments. To seek distinction, social prestige, honors, or high office
Exhibition (nExh)	To attract attention to one's person. To excite, amuse, stir, shock, thrill others. To make an impression. To be seen and heard

Table 4.1 (continued)

Need	Related actions
Cognizance (nCog)	To ask questions. To satisfy curiosity. To look, listen, inspect. To read and seek knowledge
Exposition (nExp)	To point and demonstrate. To relate facts. To give information, explain, interpret, and lecture
Understanding (nUnd)	To analyze experience, to abstract, to discriminate among concepts, to define relations, to synthesize ideas and arrive at generalizations
Play (nPlay)	To relax, amuse oneself, seek diversion and entertainment. To 'have fun,' to laugh, joke, and be merry
Sentience (nSen)	To seek and enjoy sensuous impressions such as pleasurable sights (color, light, form, movement, a beautiful face, clothes, decoration, landscapes, architecture, painting, and sculpture) and pleasurable sounds (natural sounds, human voice, poetry, and music)
Sex (nSex)	To form and further an erotic relationship. To have sexual intercourse

Table 4.2 Motivational analysis of combat abilities

Ability	Description	Motivation
Hit/hit streak	Each time a player successfully hits an enemy, the hit counter increases. This counter resets if player waits too long or receives damage from enemy attacks. If the player can collect a certain amount of hits he/she can spend the hit streak for a powerful attack	nAgg
Elf shot	Serves as ammo for the Wraith bow. This is the player's primary source of ranged attacks. Some wraith powers use this resource and it is favorable to have Elf Shots fully stocked at all times	nAgg
Weapon runes	Each killed Uruk Captain drops a weapon rune. These runes can be equipped to modify the stats of the three weapons the player owns	nAgg nCons
Focus	Focus slowdowns time during the bow aim making it easier to shoot targets	nAgg

4.2.1   Combat Abilities

These abilities allow the player to make more aggressive attacks (nAgg). There is only one power that allows the player to combine or configure objects (nCons) (Table 4.2).

4.2.2   Ranger Abilities

These abilities allow the player to make more aggressive attacks (nAgg) and to receive less damage since the player kills more effectively or stuns the enemies (nHarm). There is a power that gives the player the opportunity to overcome defeat

Table 4.3 Motivational analysis of ranger abilities

Ability	Description	Motivation
Impact	Countered enemies will be stunned or knocked down/back	nAgg
		nHarm
Strike from above	Aerial takedowns on unaware targets become lethal	nAgg
Critical strike	Doubles Hit Streak gains on well-timed attacks	nAgg
Last chance finisher	Initiate an execution on a successful Last Chance Struggle	nAgg
		nCnt
Poison	Poison grog barrels in Uruk camps and strongholds. Poisoned Uruks will either die or fight one another after drinking	nAgg
		nHarm
Throwing daggers	Throw a tiny, weak dagger that deals light damage and staggers enemies	nAgg
Brutalize *requires strike from above*	A stealth kill that terrorizes nearby enemies, forcing them to flee. Also builds Hit Streak	nAgg
		nDom
Swift finisher	Reduces time required to perform Ground Executions in combat	nAgg
Vault stun	Vaulting over an enemy will stun him	nAgg
		nHarm
Brace of daggers *requires throwing daggers*	Upgrades Throwing Daggers so that three can be thrown in quick succession	nAgg
Shoulder charge	Upgrades Dash attacks to break shields and knock enemies down	nAgg
Blade master *requires critical strike*	Reduces Hit Streak threshold for special moves from 8 to 5	nAgg
Resilience	Ability to absorb one hit without resetting the Hit Streak counter	nAgg
		nHarm
Death threat	Issue a Death Threat to a Captain or Warchief, improving the chance to earn an Epic Rune	nAcq
Critical strike II *requires blade master*	3× Hit Streak gains on well-timed attacks	nAgg
Flame of vengeance	Striking enemies after charging Talion's Hit Streak will do 2× damage	nAgg
Double charge	With a charged Hit Streak, perform two special moves instead of one	nAgg

or failure by retaliating (nCnt), a power that allows the player to terrorize nearby enemies (nDom) and a power that increases the chance of getting a rune (nAcq) (Table 4.3).

4.2.3 Wraith Abilities

These abilities allow the player to make more aggressive attacks (nAgg) and to receive less damage since the player kills more effectively or stuns the enemies (nHarm). There are seven powers used for dominating mounts (caragors or graugs) or terrorizing enemies (nDom). Since riding caragors or graugs is also a casual activity for the player, there are four powers satisfying the need for sentience (nSen). There is one power used for the need of affiliation (nAff) and another power is used for rejecting branded Uruks (nRej) and gaining runes (nAcq) (Table 4.4).

4.2.4 Upgrades

Upgrades bought via spending Mirian allow the player increase some of his/her stats. Most of these upgrades are used to make more aggressive attacks (nAgg). The rune upgrades allow the player to combine or configure objects (nCons) but depending on the runes the player uses his/her motivation varies (Table 4.5).

4.2.5 Runes

There are three types of runes in the game: sword runes, bow runes, and dagger runes. Since they resemble each other, we only analyzed sword runes (both basic and epic) in our motivational analysis. Similar to the other categories analyzed before, runes are also designed for the need for aggression (nAgg) and need for harmavoidance (nHarm) (Table 4.6).

4.3 Gaming Situations

Players with different motivations and goals experience various gaming situations that provide different incentives and punishers/reinforcers. Is there a motivational framework to analyze the basics of goal-directed behavior in computer games? Is it possible to analyze player behavior within a motivated action model? How do players make choices and why do they make these choices? This section combines the motivated action model described before with the motivational framework of Murray (1938) to answer these questions. Each gaming situation from *Shadows of Mordor* is described with appropriate incentive, goal, motivation, action, reinforcer, and punisher.

Situation 1

- *Situation*: The player randomly encounters an Uruk Captain
- *Positive Incentive*: Earning a rune
- *Goal*: Killing the captain
- *Motivation*: Achievement (nAch), Acquisition (nAcq), Aggression (nAgg)
- *Action*: Attack the captain
- *Punisher*: Uruk Captain gets promoted if the player dies
- *Punisher≥ Positive Incentive*: Possibility of a higher rune

Table 4.4 Motivational analysis of wraith abilities

Ability	Description	Motivation
Elven swiftness	Time your landings when vaulting over obstacles to gain a temporary speed boost and Hit Streak point (can be used both for chasing and running away)	nAgg nHarm
Ride caragors	Mount Caragors by jumping onto their backs from above	nDom nSen
Wraith stun	Stun enemies and follow it with a flurry of fast and deadly sword strikes	nAgg nHarm
Caragor hunter	Ability to counter and stun, then mount a charging caragor	nHarm nDom nSen
Pin in place	Arrows fired at an Uruk's legs will pin him to the ground, immobilizing him	nAgg nHarm
Shadow strike	Spend 2 Elf-Shot to teleport to a targeted enemy and knock him down	nAgg nHarm
Stealth drain	Grants the capability to drain enemies, replenishing Elf-shot and focus, without revealing the presence of Talion to other enemies	nHarm
Wraith flash	Area attack that stuns enemies, available when a Hit Streak is charged	nAgg nHarm
Combat drain	Instantly drain and terrorize an Uruk in combat, after charging a Hit Streak	nDom
Graug hunter	Stun a Graug with a sneak attack, then mount and ride it	nHarm nDom nSen
Lethal shadow strike	Lethal version of Shadow Strike. The player teleports to a nearby place, and then kills a target	nAgg nHarm
Wraith finisher	The heads of victims of Flurry kills or Drains will explode, scaring other Uruks	nDom
Brand	All Drain moves now Dominate targets, forcing them to fight for Talion	nDom nAff
Fire arrow	With a charged Hit Streak, arrows are now lit aflame before firing	nAgg
Shadow mount	Instantly mount a Graug or Caragor with Shadow Strike	nDom nHarm nSen
Wraith blast	Upgrades Wraith Stun so that enemies in a cone around your target are hit	nAgg nHarm
Dispatch	Kill all branded Uruk or monsters. Branded Uruk Captains also drop runes	nRej nAcq
Quick draw	Increase Elf-Shot charge speed	nAgg
Shadow strike chain *requires lethal shadow strike*	Chain together Shadow Strike attacks, both in or out of combat scenarios	nAgg nHarm
Wraith burn	With a charged hit streak, let out a circle of Wraith fire that kills any stunned or downed enemies	nAgg

Table 4.5 Motivational analysis of upgrades

Upgrade	Description	Motivation
Max focus upgrade	Increases focus	nAgg
Max elf shot upgrade	Increases elf shots	nAgg
Max sword rune upgrade	Increases the number of sword runes	nCons varies
Max bow rune upgrade	Increases the number of bow runes	nCons varies
Max dagger rune upgrade	Increases the number of dagger runes	nCons varies
Storm of Urfael	Charged with melee kills. Allows Talion to perform unlimited executions for 20 s. Can be extended by 10 s with the Ruination weapon rune	nAgg
Flame of Azkar	Charged with ranged kills. Allows Talion 15 s of unlimited Elf-shot, Focus and Fire Arrows. Can be extended by 10 s with the Wrath of the Eldar weapon rune	nAgg
Shadow of Acharn	Charged with stealth kills. Allows Talion to become invisible for 20 s, enabling unlimited stealth kills. Can be recharged faster with the Oathbreaker weapon rune	nAgg

In this situation, the player randomly meets an Uruk Captain. The positive incentive for killing these enemies is the runes they drop. The player's goal is to kill the enemy but his motivation could be to gain experience and advance, and/or to get a rune, and/or aggression. The punisher for this situation is that if the player dies the captain gets promoted and will become stronger but when a captain gets stronger the rune that he will drop also gets stronger so this punisher may transform into a positive incentive. Some players may get themselves killed for getting better runes from Uruk Captains.

Situation 2

- *Situation*: The player randomly encounters an Uruk Captain
- *Negative Incentive*: The captain has no exploitable weakness
- *Goal*: Avoiding the captain
- *Motivation*: Harmavoidance (nHarm)
- *Action*: Escape battle
- *Punisher*: Uruk Captain gets promoted if the player escapes
- *Punisher≥Negative Incentive*: Running away makes the next encounter harder

In this situation, the player randomly meets an Uruk Captain. Enemies usually have a weakness so that the player can come with a strategy to defeat them but sometimes a captain may have no exploitable weakness. So, the player's goal is to run away and his/her motivation is Harmavoidance. But if the player runs away after the encounter started, the captain will get promoted and thus the punisher may transform into a negative incentive because the next time the player encounters the same captain the battle will be harder (Table 4.7).

Table 4.6 Motivational analysis of sword runes

Rune	Description	Motivation
Basic		
Blade master	$(25 + (Level \times 3))$ % chance to recover full health when a Hit Streak reaches 30	nHarm
For vengeance	Increases melee damage by $(10 + Level)$ % during a high Hit Streak (30+)	nAgg
Grim resolve	$(Level)$ % defense versus ranged attacks	nHarm
Know no pain	$(10 + Level)$ % chance to recover +5 health on any kill	nHarm
Power of earth	Recovers $(25 + (Level \times 3))$ % Focus on ground execution	nAgg
Quick to anger	$(10 + Level)$ % chance to recover +5 health on each Critical Strike	nHarm
Savage onslaught	Increase melee damage by $(10 + Level)$ % at mid-Hit Streak range (15–29)	nAgg
Smite	Recover $(25 + (Level \times 3))$ % Focus on a Flurry kill	nAgg
Strength from courage	Recover $(Level)$ % health on a Flurry kill	nHarm
Epic		
Bones of the earth	Recover +3 Elf Shot on a Flurry kill	nAgg
Burning pitch	15 % chance to ignite enemies on a counter	nAgg
Elven grace	50 % chance to reduce melee damage received by half	nHarm
Evenstar	Recover full Focus when a Hit Streak is charged	nAgg
Foe hammer	Recover +2 Elf Shot with Combat Executions	nAgg
Mighty rage	Increases the stun and knockdown durations on melee attacks	nDom
		nHarm
Ruination	Increases the Storm of Urfael duration by 10 s	nAgg
Stand and fight	Do 2× sword damage when Talion's health goes below 25 %	nCnt
		nAgg
Storm of battle	Increases all sword damage by 50 %	nAgg
The end comes	Uruks' heads will explode on Wraith Blast kills	nDom
The undying	Recover all Focus and Elf-shot on any Last Chance success	nAgg
Tower of defense	Increase Hit Streak reset time +10 s	nAgg
Wraith and ruin	Increase stun/knockdown durations of Wraith Flash	nHarm

Situation 3

- *Situation*: The player meets a clumsy Uruk Captain
- *Positive Incentive*: Clumsy Uruks can be branded
- *Goal*: Branding the Uruk Captain
- *Motivation*: Dominance (nDom), Affiliation (nAff)
- *Action*: Try to grapple the Uruk Captain
- *Reinforcer*: The Uruk Captain is the bodyguard of a Warchief

In this situation, the player meets an Uruk Captain with a weakness named clumsy. When an Uruk is clumsy, he can be grappled and branded in full health. Branding grants the player the power to dominate any Uruk soldier, Captain, or

Table. 4.7 An Uruk Captain with a single weakness, immune to almost all player powers

	Weaknesses
	Fear of burning Becomes terrified when he burns
	Strengths
	Combat master Invulnerable to Combat attacks and Finishers
	Invulnerable to stealth Cannot be damaged by Stealth Takedowns
	Invulnerable to ranged Cannot be damaged by your Ranged attacks
	Monster slayer Able to kill monsters quickly, and resistant to their attacks
	Inspiring presence Nearby Uruks are inspired to attack simultaneously
	Ambusher Launches ambushes against his enemies
	Rapid Attack Multiple attacks that must be individually Countered
	Heavy Attack High-damage melee attack, cannot be Countered
	Jump attack Leaps far while striking

Warchief, granting total control over them. The player can then direct them to aid him in combat and to kill other Uruk soldiers or Captains. So, the player decides to brand this Uruk and his/her motivation is Dominance (nDom) and Affiliation (nAff). The reinforcer of this situation is that the Uruk Captain is the bodyguard of a Warchief. So, if the player successfully brands this enemy, he/she can direct the bodyguard captain to kill his Warchief to become the new branded Warchief.

Situation 4

- *Situation*: The player has too many branded Uruks
- *Positive Incentive*: Killing branded Uruks also gives runes
- *Positive Incentive*: One of the branded captains has stealth vulnerability
- *Goal*: Killing the branded Uruk Captain with a stealth finisher
- *Motivation*: Acquisition (nAcq), Rejection (nRej)
- *Action*: Killing the branded Uruk Captain
- *Reinforcer*: Receiving a dagger rune

In this situation, the player has too many branded Uruk Captains so they are expendable. Since killing the branded Uruks also gives runes to the player, he/she decides to attack one of the Uruk Captains who has stealth vulnerability. If the player exploits this weakness and kills the captain with a stealth finisher, he/she will get a dagger rune because using vulnerabilities ensures the rune type. The player's motivation could be Acquisition and/or Rejection (to abandon or exclude a friend). And getting a dagger rune by exploiting a weakness reinforces the player's need for information. If the player knows the weaknesses of the enemies or friends, he/she can exploit them to get the rune he/she wants.

Situation 5

- *Situation*: The player meets a high level Uruk Captain
- *Positive Incentive*: Killing high level Uruks drop better runes
- *Positive Incentive*: Threatened Uruks will have a higher chance to drop epic runes
- *Positive Incentive*: The Uruk Captain fears Caragors
- *Negative Incentive*: Threatened Uruks will be better protected
- *Goal*: Receiving an epic rune
- *Motivation*: Acquisition (nAcq)
- *Action*: Threatening the captain, riding a caragor, and engaging in battle
- *Reinforcer*: Receiving an epic rune

In this situation, the player meets a high level Uruk Captain. The player knows that the higher the level of the Uruk the better the rune he drops. The player also has the Death Threat ability which allows him/her to "threaten" a Captain or Warchief, resulting in a high chance of dropping epic runes, but also increasing the target's power, and their forces' numerical strength. But the high level Uruk also has a weakness, he fears the aggressive but tamable bestial species named Caragors. So, the player first issues a death threat and then finds a caragor to ride into the battle because he/she knows that the Uruk Captain will be terrified when he sees the caragor. Killing the captain and receiving the epic rune reinforces the player's belief that issuing death threats increases the chance of receiving epic runes.

Situation 6

- *Situation*: There is an Uruk Captain which the player has no Intel on
- *Negative Incentive*: Uruk's strengths are active even if you don't know them
- *Positive Incentive*: There is a Worm nearby

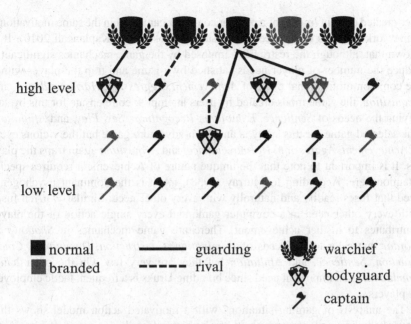

high level

low level

normal | ────── guarding | warchief
branded | - - - - - rival | bodyguard
| | captain

Fig. 4.2 Nemesis system comprised of warchiefs, bodyguards, and captains

- *Goal*: Gaining more information about the Captain
- *Motivation*: Cognizance (nCog), Harmavoidance (nHarm)
- *Action*: Interrogating the worm to get Intel about the captain
- *Reinforcer*: Learn the strengths and weaknesses of the captain

In this situation, there is an Uruk Captain that the player has no Intel on. If the player does not know anything about the weaknesses and strengths of an Uruk, he/she has to try finishers, ranged moves and dodges early in the fight to learn more about his/her enemy but this may be risky. The player's motivation is to avoid harm (harmavoidance) and this can be accomplished by learning more about the captain (cognizance). When the player investigates his/her surroundings he/she notices that there is a worm nearby. Worms are specially marked Uruks that glow green when the player enters the Wraith World and they have Intel on other Uruks. So, the player interrogates the worm to learn the strengths and weaknesses of the captain so that he/she will be able to come up with a strategy to defeat him. This course of action also reinforces the player's belief that interrogating worm Uruks may be useful. Knowing your enemy is the key to dominate the Nemesis system of the game (Fig. 4.2).

4.4 Conclusion

The motivational framework in this chapter has been applied to an RPG before and the psychological needs are investigated by defining the driving game mechanics behind them (Bostan and Kaplancali 2009). The same authors also analyzed user-created content (mods) of a popular computer game within the same motivational framework in terms of the needs they satisfy (Bostan and Kaplancali 2010). It is shown that, although the restrictions imposed by the game mechanics significantly reduce the number of player needs satisfied by a game and trap the player within the common motivational cycle of *Achievement*, *Aggression*, *Harmavoidance*, and *Acquisition*, the game mods created by users attempt to compensate for this by satisfying the needs of *Sentience*, *Exhibition*, *Recognition*, *Sex*, *Play*, and *Affiliation*. The selected game for this study is an action-adventure game but the vicious cycle of *Achievement*, *Aggression*, *Harmavoidance*, and *Acquisition* again traps the players. It is important to note that the unique nature of Achievement requires special attention here. According to Murray (1938), nAch is the dominant psychogenic need that fuses readily and naturally with every other need. Similarly, nAch fuses with every other need in a computer game and every single action of the player contributes to his/her achievement. There are game mechanics in *Shadows of Mordor* that cater to the needs of *Domination*, *Construction*, *Dominance*, *Counteraction*, *Sentience*, and *Affiliation* but they are very few. On the other hand, *Dominance* is an important need since branding Uruks is a frequent tactic employed by players.

The analysis of gaming situations with a motivated action model shows that player behavior in a computer game can be better described in terms of *incentives*, *goals*, *motivations*, *actions*, *reinforcers*, and *punishers*. Players may have to ponder over a situation and then make a decision based on the strength or appeal of an incentive. Lewin (1936) described this phenomenon as a psychological force, which is dependent on both the valence (strength) of the incentive and the psychological distance to the incentive. Objects or activities that have a positive valence attract the individual, and are sought and wanted. On the other hand, those that have negative valence repel the individual, and are avoided and not wanted. Objects or activities that are closer are approached more easily than those that are far away. In computer games, the valence of incentives is usually reflected in the rewards the player receives. Short-term goals have more immediately achievable rewards and long-term goals provide the overall reward structure of the game. As the player progresses, the positive valence of objects or activities also increases. The reinforcers and punishers also provide a feedback mechanism for goal-directed behavior and affect the player's future choices. And the motivational framework of Murray (1938), when applied with the motivated action model, perfectly describes the anatomy of a player choice. The motivations or the needs of the player determine the action toward a goal.

References

Bandura A, Cervone D (1983) Self-evaluative and self-efficacy mechanisms governing the motivational effects of goal systems. J Pers Soc Psychol 45:1017–1028
Bolles RC (1975) Theory of motivation. Harper & Row, New York
Bostan B (2009) Player motivations: a psychological perspective. ACM Comput Entertain 7(2). http://dl.acm.org/citation.cfm?doid=1541895.1541902

Bostan B, Kaplancali U (2009) Explorations in player motivations: game mechanics. Proceedings of GAMEON 2009, Düsseldorf, Germany, 2009

Bostan B, Kaplancali U (2010) Explorations in player motivations: game mods. Proceedings of GAMEON-ASIA 2010, Shanghai, China, 2010

Heckhausen J, Heckhausen H (2005) Motivation and action. Cambridge University Press, Cambridge

Lewin K (1936) Principles of topological psychology (trans: Heider F, Heider G). McGraw-Hill, New York

Logan FA (1960) Incentive. Yale University Press, New Haven

Logan FA, Wagner AR (1965) Reward and punishment. Allyn & Bacon, Boston

Maslow AH (1943) A theory of human motivation. Psychol Rev 50(4):370–396

Maslow AH (1968) Toward a psychology of being. D. Van Nostrand Company, New York

McDougall W (1908) An introduction to social psychology. Methuen, London

Murray HA (1938) Explorations in personality. Oxford University Press, Oxford

Skinner BF (1938) The behavior of organisms. Appleton-Century-Crofts, New York

Skinner BF (1953) Science and human behavior. Macmillan, New York

Staddon JER, Simmelhag VL (1971) The "superstition" experiment: a reexamination of its implications for the principles of adaptive behavior. Psychol Rev 78:3–43

Chapter 5
Designing and Playing to Protest: Looking Back to Gezi Games

Tonguc Ibrahim Sezen and Digdem Sezen

Abstract This chapter is about the design, development, and perception of video-games produced during Gezi Park Protests in 2013 as a form of civic participation. The chapter first outlines the production history of these games which came to a sudden end due to the changes in the political atmosphere. A detailed description is given of the theoretical approaches on design and use of political games and news-games in the following section. Based on these approaches, five games produced during the protests were tested by a small group of participants.

Keywords Gezi Protests • Current event games • Newsgames • Civic engagement

5.1 Introduction

Many forms of new media including micro blogs, video sharing platforms, and social networks have been used by activists and protesters during recent wide spread public protests all around the world (Gerbaudo 2012). This was also the case during the Istanbul Gezi Park Protests of Summer 2013. Like their predecessors in other countries, the contents created by the protestors in Turkey too were foremost a means to organize the occupation and spread the political discourse; but they were also humorous and playful (Dagtas 2013; Ogun Emre et al. 2014; Colak 2014; Varol 2014). Among the collection of collective, decentralized, and creative artifacts such as examples of street art, short films, and online banners; several videogames too have been created as a show of support to the protests and a way of discussing its reasons.

T.I. Sezen, Ph.D. (✉)
Department of Digital Game Design, Istanbul Bilgi University, Istanbul, Turkey
e-mail: tonguc.sezen@bilgi.edu.tr

D. Sezen, Ph.D.
Department of Radio, Television and Film, Istanbul University, Istanbul, Turkey
e-mail: dsezen@istanbul.edu.tr

© Springer International Publishing Switzerland 2016
B. Bostan (ed.), *Gamer Psychology and Behavior*, International Series
on Computer Entertainment and Media Technology,
DOI 10.1007/978-3-319-29904-4_5

Like most artistic production by the Gezi Park protestors (Colak 2014), these videogames were mostly produced in a very short time and in an unorganized and collective fashion. Designed by individuals and independent game development communities using open source resources, they were short and simple, and were distributed freely online for anyone to experience their designers' depiction of and personal perspectives on the ongoing events. These games were soon followed by a smaller number of commercial videogames depicting Gezi Park Protests. By the end of August 2013, the total number of videogames referring to the protests had reached 21. Unfortunately, like most online content created during the events, half of these games are now inaccessible. Either the websites they were distributed from are offline or they were removed from application stores by their developers for unknown reasons. Today, 2 years after the protests, what is left of the videogames created during Gezi Park Protests in 2013 is a collection of 10 games still accessible and playable online. These interactive artifacts document the creative notions and political views of their designers at the time of their creation.

This chapter focuses on a smaller subset of the remaining Gezi Park videogames and explores them as possible embodiments of several concepts proposed and discussed by digital game scholars regarding the civic use of digital games over the past 10 years. This notion requires an understanding of how they were created, how they work, and how they are expected to be perceived by players. In this regard in the following section, we will first explore videogame production during Gezi Park Protest. The next section will establish a theoretical basis for a study of Gezi Park videogames through the lenses of digital game studies. In the last section, we will analyze the findings of a small sized player study on the perception of selected examples by today's players. In the conclusion, we will evaluate our findings.

5.2 Gezi Park Protests and Videogames

Istanbul Gezi Park Protests refer to nationwide demonstrations and civil unrest in Turkey which started at the end of May 2013 as a reaction to the violent crackdown of a small environmentalist protest against the redevelopment plans of the Taksim area (which included the removal of Gezi Park, one of the last green spaces in central Istanbul) by the police. Initial reaction of tens of thousands of people marching toward Taksim Square and clashing with the police resulted with the withdrawal of the police in June 1 and the occupation of Gezi Park which not only acted as the center for the protests but also served as a forum for political discussion and a platform for different types of creative forms of protest, until its takeover by riot police in June 15. Although they started without a centralized leadership or any definite political goals beyond preventing the destruction of Gezi Park, fueled by the harsh response of the police forces, concerns regarding the policies of the ruling Justice and Development Party on issues such as civil liberties and freedom of expression, and the initial failure of mainstream media in reporting the events (Tastan 2013; KONDA 2014), protests spread to several cities of Turkey within weeks. The government reacted to these developments with a massive deployment of riot police.

After months of clashes, resulting with high numbers of injuries and several deaths among civilians, protest faded in late August 2013 (Amnesty International 2013).

From the first days, besides more traditional forms of protest such as occupations, rallies, and sit-ins, protestors used productive methods to be informed, to express themselves, and spread their messages in humorous ways, which included prose and poetry; paintings, graffiti, and sculptures; music and performance; and also digital content such as blogs and banners (Colak 2014; Ogun Emre et al. 2014; Koenitz 2014). In early June 2013 during the occupation of Gezi Park, the unofficial digital game developer community Game Developers @ Turkey announced the organization of an event called #GeziJAM. It followed the game design marathon model "global-game-jam" in which game designers were asked to develop a functioning prototype within 48 h (Global Game Jam 2015). On their current website, the group declares their reasons for organizing the event as their support to the goals of the protests and their willingness to show their solidarity by the means of game design (Game Developers @ Turkey 2015). On their now offline invitation page, they had listed possible themes as disinformation, police violence, democracy, and freedom of media; and also noted that there would be no restrictions on the subjects as long as they weren't promoting violent acts. "If…" they had announced, "…you have something you want to say about the events and if you believe you can say it best through a game, this is your chance" (Game Developers @ Turkey 2013a). According to one of the organizers, Ali Bati, #GeziJAM by itself had also reflected the ideals of the Gezi Park Protests in its collaborative nature since designers were expected to support each other during the development process. In addition, unlike other game-jams Bati noted, #GeziJAM also had no strict time restriction due to the active participation of game developers to the protests (Bati, cited in Kentel 2013). At the end of the announced deadline of June 13, merely 2 days before the clearance of the Gezi Park by the police, 12 videogames were released online for anyone to play freely. Their introduction was praising the peaceful atmosphere in the occupied Gezi Park and reflected hopes for a democratic resolution to the protests all over the country (Game Developers @ Turkey 2013b). From the 12 videogames produced during #GeziJAM, only 3 are online and accessible today: *Path of the Trees*, *Resist Auntie*, and *Occupygezi,* all of which will be analyzed in the following sections.

Although #GeziJAM was the only collective game development activity organized for the support of Gezi Park Protests, individuals and small teams outside the Game Developers @ Turkey community too developed and released videogames on different platforms for similar purposes between June and August 2013. These games can be listed as follows: *Pac-Chapull, Direnistan, Capulcu, The Capulcu, Resist Gezi Park,* and *Everyday I'm Chapulling*. Among these games, only *Pac-Chapull, Resist Gezi Park, Direnistan*, and *Everyday I'm Chapulling* are still online today. *Resist Gezi Park* had relatively limited access from day one since it was only released for mobile platforms and the multiplayer game *Direnistan* is accessible but without a player base currently unplayable.

While the videogames listed above were released as a form of protest, other games depicting Gezi Park Protests as their setting were also released for commercial purposes during the same period. Starting right after the police takeover of the

Gezi Park in mid-June 2013 and continuing till late 2013, Turkish gaming site Oyuncini.com which is offering short casual games to its' customers started to release simple videogames either depicting or referring to Gezi Park Protests. Including *Gezi Parki İsyani*, *Duran Adam*, and *Marmaray Seysi* (which only referred to the events through the use of a song recorded during the protests in its' soundtrack), these games started with promotional clips of the website and offered score sharing options for social media channels which included links directing possible customers to Oyuncini.com. Thus, whether or not their designers supported the protests the games themselves acted as marketing devices. In late 2013, the Korean game developer S&T Play released a commercial platform runner called *Chapulling* for mobile platforms. The game used imagery of Gezi Park Protests such as characters resembling known protestors and Taksim Square as the location; yet featuring in-app purchases the game was clearly a commercial product. By 2015, it was no longer listed in application stores. The last videogame produced in 2013 on Gezi Park Protests was neither a commercial product nor was it a direct part of the protest effort. Designed by film director Inan Temelkuran and digital artist Hartmut Koenitz, *Occupy Istanbul* was an interactive digital narrative exhibited in late 2013 as an interactive art piece. It allowed players to explore different aspects of the protests through controlling a protestor in the early days of the events (ICIDS 2013). Using images and videos collected from social networks, it has been described by its designers as a game engaging "several topics pertaining to the relationship of the individual and the political sphere, including civic obedience, resistance against state power and citizen media" (Koenitz 2014). Being an exhibition piece, Occupy Istanbul had a relatively limited reach.

Despite being covered by the press (Ive 2013; Kaya 2013; Kentel 2013), and being discussed in contemporary arts festivals (Gunhan 2013), it's hard to tell how these videogames were perceived by people who played them at that time. *Resist Gezi Park* is still listed in Google Play Store and has a 3.5 star rating based on 87 reviews. A discussion thread following a news article on #GeziJam (Isal 2013) on the official website of the Turkish gaming magazine Oyungezer provides another angle on the perception of games and game-jams as a way of protest. Out of 219 comments (all posted in 2013) listed in the thread, only a handful refers directly to #GeziJAM and none to its products. Instead, commentators defend their own political positions toward the protests and reject any opposing arguments. Interestingly while there are some praises among them, most of the small number of comments mentioning the game-jam actually criticize Oyungezer for reporting such a "political subject." Games and game sites these commentators argue should be nonpolitical.

5.2.1   Key Concepts to Understand Gezi Park Videogames

Over the years, several concepts such as "serious games" (Ferdig 2014; Clément 2014; Blumberg et al. 2013), "political games" (Lerner 2014; Sicart 2014), "activist games" (Flanagan 2009), "newsgames" (Frasca 2004; Treanor and Mateas 2009;

Sicart 2009; Bogost et al. 2010), and "current event games" (Bogost et al. 2010) have been suggested by game scholars to discuss games designed to explore, criticize, and even provoke social, economic, or political subjects. Overlapping on some aspects and diverging on others, these concepts provide a theoretical framework through which the design, development, and experience of Gezi Park videogames can be evaluated.

Being produced for a reason beyond entertainment is one of the key features of all the concepts listed above but more so for the broadest one of them; "serious games." Richard E. Ferdig describes a serious game as a game "that has been designed for a reason other than to just entertain, regardless of the field, motivation, or context for which it was created" (Ferdig 2014, p. 319). Supporting an ongoing protest as in the games produced during Gezi Park Protests definitely falls under this category. Yet, as this definition suggests serious games is an umbrella term which covers a wide range of different types of games including educational and training games (Clément 2014, p. 202). One of these sub categories, serious games encouraging civic engagement, may seem like a relevant reference point though, since they aim to "promote acknowledgment of and action directed toward issues of public concern" (Blumberg et al. 2013, p. 341). In their study on the civic potential of videogames, Kahne et al. (2009) too argue that videogames may be used by gaming communities to discuss, debate, and learn about current events and social issues. Yet they also underline the need for an informed discussion in an open climate to reach these goals (Kahne et al. 2009). In other words, games fostering civic engagement require an analytical thought process and well-planned design and development circle to be affective; which none of the games produced during Gezi Protests had for several reasons such as time restrictions.

Another concept which may be helpful to understand games produced during the Gezi Park Protest is "activist games." Similar to serious games, according to game scholar Mary Flanagan, "activist games can be characterized by their emphasis on social issues, education, and, occasionally, intervention" (Flanagan 2009, p. 13). In other words, the goals of their designers and their intended uses play a key role in defining activist games. In her book *Critical Play: Radical Game Design,* Flanagan gives several examples of activist games ranging from physical games to board games and to videogames which have been designed to argue for or to protest against different social or political subjects. These subjects can be found embedded to different game design elements such as themes, narratives, settings, characters, game mechanics, or winning states. The latter two, according to Flanagan (2009), are rarer in practice and more desirable from a critical design point of view. As one can expect, most physical activist games Flanagan analyzed in her book were played as forms of protest on the streets by protestors. In other words, they were part of an event in a specific time and space. Most videogames she analyzed on the other hand were either individual artistic pieces or promotional games supported by nonprofits or other organizations to explain or criticize a social or political issue which was either a long running problem of the society the designers were part of or a large-scale problem in another society which needed global attention, meaning they were designed with a temporal, critical, and in some cases geographical distance to their subjects. Among games depicting Gezi Park Protests, only *Occupy Istanbul* had such a distance to its subject.

According to game scholar Miguel Sicart, a specific context is one of the key factors in defining a game or a playful action as activist or political. He gives an evasive street game designed for protesters against riot control techniques as an example which can only be considered political if played against the riot police (Sicart 2014). According to Flanagan (2009), as Internet and social networks have turned into cultural spaces of the twenty-first century, games played or distributed online have also turned into spaces where political change can occur. Tracing the roots of activist games to the anti-corporate protests in Seattle in 1999, the Italian guerilla videogame developing group Molleindustria (2004) too considers online distribution of games with political agendas as the next logical step in spreading political ideas to larger audiences. According to them, these games can either have complex game mechanics reflecting critical points, or be designed based on simple popular classic games in order to draw attention to other informative material or online activist communities. In regard to the latter, Sicart points out a danger he argues most contemporary political videogames face; "the "political" [video] game…" he says "…is just a (single) player game that addresses a political theme of the moment and then rapidly vanishes from the public scene" (Sicart 2014, p. 73). Most videogames based on Gezi Park Protest were produced in a very short time, within a special context. They were designed and meant to be played as a form of support to the occupation of the Gezi Park; but this context suddenly ceased to exist due to the takeover of the park by the riot police. We can never be certain on how these videogames would perform if the political environment had continued to exist in the manner their developers had envisioned. Would they vanish or become iconic symbols of the protest? Whatever the answer may be, we can argue that their circulation has been interrupted and they never really had the chance to be evaluated by their then potential audiences.

In this respect, as a creative process #GeziJAM reflects some of the aspects of what game scholar and designer Gonzalo Frasca (2004) calls "forum videogames." Inspired by Augusto Boal's concept of "forum theatre," forum videogames can be described as communal workshops in which participants create videogames to discuss real-life situations. Instead of expert designers or programmers, these participants are expected to be anyone who is affected by or wants to understand and discuss the issue at hand. Despite Sicart's criticism mentioned above, in order to overcome their possible limitations in technical expertise, Frasca suggests to design videogames in such forums through modifying preexistent templates based on classic videogames such as *Space Invaders* (1978) or *Pac-Man* (1980). Since the main goal of forum videogames is not to find absolute solutions but rather trigger discussion, once shared with the community, videogames developed in these forums are expected to be open to discussion and further modification by other participants to explore multiple and alternative points of view. In other words, (a) discussion of the problem, (b) game design through modification and remaking, (c) further discussion of the suggested point of view in the game, and (d) further modification of the game to explore alternate views are the repeating phases of forum videogames as a critical and creative method. To some extent, we may say that after fulfilling the first two of these phases as an example of forum videogames, #GeziJAM's progress had been interrupted.

While the concept of forum videogames explains how videogames may be produced on political or social issues by the people directly affected by them, it does little to describe the features of videogames which would be produced during such an event. Another concept coined by Frasca, "newsgames," may be helpful in doing so (Newsgaming 2003). Frasca characterizes newsgames as the videogame equivalents of traditional political cartoons, which are "short, controversial satirical pieces that convey biased ideological messages" (Newsgaming 2003). Based on this, later scholars defined an ideal newsgame as a videogame which takes an editorial position toward an ongoing issue (Treanor and Mateas 2009). Discussing the political nature of this editorial position, Sicart described newsgames as "an editorialized, not persuasive genre of political games or serious games, developed in connection to a specific piece of news" (Sicart 2009). Based on an analysis of different types of intersections between videogames and journalism, Bogost et al. (2010) on the other hand suggested to use newsgames as an umbrella term and proposed "current event games" to describe games discussed by Frasca, Sicart, Trenor, and Mateas. Current event games according to them were "short, bite-sized works, usually embedded in Web sites, used to convey small bits of news information or opinion" (Bogost et al. 2010, p. 13). In all these different approaches, there were several common criteria defining newsgames among others with short production circles and more or less reactionary nature. These criteria can be used as a basis to analyze and discuss games produced during Gezi Park Protests from an analytical point of view.

Newsgames are produced within a temporal proximity to the news stories they cover. This is called the timeliness of a newsgame (Bogost et al. 2010). Newsgames are expected to be released before the stories they are based on become irrelevant for the society, or reach saturation. Yet if a story has universal characteristics or continues to be important for a society, an effective newsgame covering it can be produced regardless of the time distance to the story (Treanor and Mateas 2009). In fact, newsgames are expected only to remain in circulation as long as the story they cover is relevant. This temporal extension though makes it harder to distinguish between newsgames and activist games; the current event aspect should be taken into consideration if such a distinction is relevant for an analysis.

Newsgames tend to have very short production circles. One strategy to ease this process is, like in forum videogames, to borrow or modify mechanics of older, known videogames (Sicart 2009). Newsgames following this approach are easy to learn and play, and thus direct their players quickly to their content (Bogost et al. 2010). Alongside temporal restrictions, newsgames also face logistical challenges. To reach wider audiences in time, they have to be short, compact, and easily distributable online (Bogost et al. 2010). Videogames produced during Gezi Park Protests shared most of these temporal, logistical, and technical restrictions and challenges during their production and distribution. But game scholars have also defined several characteristics regarding newsgames' content and design.

Unlike partisan games, such as election games supporting a candidate, (Bogost and Frasca 2007) which aim to shift or reassure the political beliefs of their players, newsgames intend to participate in the public debate by representing different perspectives and arguments to an audience to whom the subject they cover is relevant (Sicart 2009). Newsgames are biased toward an editorial position and this position aims to provide a specific commentary on a specific subject or problem, and if possible implies a solution (Treanor and Mateas 2009). In this regard Bogost et al. (2010) use the term "editorial games" to describe such current event games. Editorial games attempt to persuade their players toward their arguments through utilizing different design elements (Bogost et al. 2010, p. 15). As in activist games, these design elements may vary, but the translation of the editorial position into game play is regarded (Sicart 2009; Treanor and Mateas 2009; Bogost et al. 2010) the most effective way of communicating the operations of the ideas the designers want to bring forward in the public discourse. Videogames produced to support the Gezi Park Protests were politically motivated for sure. Yet like the Gezi Park Protests themselves, they were not under the influence of an ideological or political superstructure which motivated and directed them toward a specific goal. Produced by individuals and an independent collective, they were far away from being the products of a partisan act. This independence though also resulted with the lack of a well-defined editorial line. Reflecting the mood and political arguments on the streets, they were to a certain degree impulsive. In this regard, we can argue that Gezi Park games were the newsgame or current event game equivalent of citizen journalism (Allan 2013), which is characterized by the temporarily content production of ordinary individuals during a time of crisis.

5.2.2 Evaluating Gezi Park Videogames

Gezi Park videogames were remarkable for being produced as personal commentaries on an ongoing political protest intended to be shared and evaluated by the public, and also for not being able to reach this goal due to the social turmoil following the sudden crackdown of this protest. Two years after this sudden interruption, we wanted to evaluate what has remained of these games. Sharing aspects of activist games and current event games, how did they construct their political positions? How would they be perceived by players as political texts, even after 2 years? Did their designers use common game mechanics with new imagery or tried to create new mechanics to express their views? Would they represent the idea of videogames as political artifacts well and encourage similar productions among players? To answer these questions, we invited 30 players to play a selected set of videogames produced during the Gezi Park Protest and then to answer a questioner regarding each one. Politically they have declared themselves against the removal of the Gezi Park which had sparked the protests. Among the 30 players 19 had actively participated to the protests and 12 of them had also produced some type of digital content to support the protests. While 7 of them were familiar with the concepts of activist games or newsgames, none of them had heard of the videogames produced during the Gezi Park Protests before. We have chosen our games to represent the idea of videogame production as a form of civic engagement; in this respect they had to be noncommercial. For practical reasons, they also had to have no platform restrictions and to be still playable as single player games. Only 5 of the 10 currently online Gezi Park videogames fitted to these criteria. These games were *Path of the Trees*, *Resist Auntie*, *Occupygezi*, *Pac-Chapull*, and *Everyday I'm Chapulling*.

The games varied in their design and the points they made about the Gezi Park Protests. *Path of the Trees* took inspiration from the environmental concerns behind the protests. It was a turn-based strategy game where the goal was to form a path of trees from one end to another of an empty map divided into squares. As the player planted these squares turn by turn, the AI-controlled opponent built immoveable concrete obstacles to block her way. While the game could be won by reaching the top end of the map, for a higher score players had to cover as much space as possible with trees. In the 2D platform game *Resist Auntie,* players controlled an elderly woman walking on the streets with the help of a stick during the protest. The game was probably inspired by images of similar women in Gezi Park taken by the press. While the effects of the police intervention could be observed in the game, the player could only interact with two types of protestors. She could either help the ones affected by tear gas, or hit the ones damaging their surroundings with her stick. This distinction between "good" and "bad" behaving protestors reflected the notion of peaceful protest despite the violent tactics of the riot police. *Occupygezi* led the player control a police officer who fired tear gas canisters toward the protestors. While the player gained points called "baksheesh" for each protestor affected by the gas, each affected protestor also spawned additional protestors marching toward the player. *Occupygezi* was a game which could only be lost by the player. One could argue that the game represented the mood during the first days of the protests, which led to the withdrawal of the police from Taksim Square and Gezi Park. As its name suggests, *Pac-Chapull* was a Pac-Man (1980) clone in which the ghosts were replaced with characters representing riot police and the media not willing to report the protests; and Pac-Man with a protestor who could equip himself with a gasmask. Like *Occupygezi*, one could argue that *Pac-Chapull* too was inspired by the first days of the protests during which protestors not only clashed with the police but also were disappointed with the failure of the mainstream media in reporting the events. *Everyday I'm Chapulling* was a strategy game on gaining public support though protests. The player controlled a protestor walking on the streets of Istanbul while also fleeing the riot police using teargas. She gained public support from each building she passes by within a limited number turns. The game had five different endings based on the public support she had gained, ranging from a continuation of government policies to the installation of a new government in the upcoming elections. To evaluate these games, we asked each player play each game twice and then asked them to answer a questioner.

We first wanted to know how genuinely these games represented the protests in the eyes of the players. When asked if the games represented their personal experiences during the protests (see Table 5.1), the agreement rate among the players who had participated in the protests was above 30 % in all games; games featuring tear-gas usage by the police had more than 50 % agreement rate. Highest disagreement

Table 5.1 "The game represented my personal experiences during Gezi Park Protests," answered by players who had participated in the protests

	Strongly agree (%)	Agree (%)	Neither agree nor disagree (%)	Disagree (%)	Strongly disagree (%)
Path of the Trees	11	25	32	21	11
Resist Auntie	16	42	20	11	11
Occupygezi	16	41	31	6	6
Pac-Chapull	5	32	37	10	16
Everyday I'm Chapulling	20	32	32	16	0

Table 5.2 "The game represented Gezi Park Protests in general," answered by players who had not participated in the protests

	Strongly agree (%)	Agree (%)	Neither agree nor disagree (%)	Disagree (%)	Strongly disagree (%)
Path of the Trees	0	18	27	45	10
Resist Auntie	0	37	45	18	0
Occupygezi	0	28	36	36	0
Pac-Chapull	0	9	73	18	0
Everyday I'm Chapulling	10	27	18	27	18

rates were given by the players to the *Pac-Chapull* and *Path of the Trees,* with 26 % and 32 %, respectively.

When players who did not participate in the protests were asked a similar question regarding the representation of Gezi Park Protests in general (see Table 5.2), they seemed to concentrate in the center with lower strong reaction rates. Nevertheless some answers were noteworthy. The environmentalist *Path of the Trees* had 55 % disagreement rate as a representation of the protests. *Resist Auntie* featuring a protagonist who was not identified as a protestor and *Everyday I'm Chapulling* which goal involved gaining the support of the people who were not on the streets had both 37 % agreement rates.

Exposing causes, showing new perspectives, and offering solution are key functions of newsgames or current event games in creating civic discussions. In this regard we asked whether or not the games explained the causes of Gezi Park Protests (see Table 5.3); to both participants of the Gezi events and to the players who did not participated to the protests. *The Path of Trees* had the highest agreement rates with 47 % in total. Considering the topic of the game, this result was fairly expected. *Everyday I'm Chapulling* had also a 46 % agreement rate. Although the gameplay did not refer to any specific cause, in its five different endings the game had exposed government policies as the source for the protests. Also, the games focusing on police violence had relatively higher rates among Gezi participants.

According to the players, none of the games was bringing up a novel perspective regarding the Gezi events (see Table 5.4). But the two games came a bit forward with their agreement rates, *Pac-Chapull* with 17 % and *Resist Auntie* with 20 % in total. *Pac-Chapull*'s critique toward the role of media, and *Resist Auntie*'s portrayal

Table 5.3 The game explains the political causes of Gezi Park Protests

	Participated in Gezi Park Protests	Strongly agree (%)	Agree (%)	Neither agree nor disagree (%)	Disagree (%)	Strongly disagree (%)
Path of the Trees	Yes	26	26	16	21	11
	No	9	27	9	46	9
	Total	20	27	13	30	10
Resist Auntie	Yes	16	21	26	16	21
	No	0	9	9	73	9
	Total	10	17	20	36	17
Occupygezi	Yes	21	26	21	21	11
	No	0	19	36	36	9
	Total	14	23	26	28	9
Pac-Chapull	Yes	5	32	26	16	21
	No	0	18	36	46	0
	Total	3	27	30	27	13
Everyday I'm Chapulling	Yes	26	26	21	21	6
	No	0	36	0	45	19
	Total	16	30	13	30	10

Table 5.4 The game provided new perspectives regarding the Gezi Park Protests

	Participated in Gezi Park Protests	Strongly agree (%)	Agree (%)	Neither agree nor disagree (%)	Disagree (%)	Strongly disagree (%)
Path of the Trees	Yes	0	11	32	32	25
	No	0	9	27	45	19
	Total	0	10	30	37	23
Resist Auntie	Yes	5	21	26	11	37
	No	0	9	27	55	9
	Total	3	17	26	27	27
Occupygezi	Yes	0	0	48	26	26
	No	0	9	18	55	18
	Total	0	3	38	38	21
Pac-Chapull	Yes	0	22	11	32	35
	No	0	9	28	45	18
	Total	0	17	17	37	29
Everyday I'm Chapulling	Yes	5	16	16	42	21
	No	0	0	18	73	9
	Total	4	11	18	49	18

of diversity among protesters might be the reason for its different status. We also found out that around half of the Gezi Protests participants, 48 %, were ambivalent about whether *Occupy Gezi* game opens up new perspectives or not. The option of controlling the virtual police against virtual representations of themselves might have led to this ambivalence.

Table 5.5 The game offers solutions regarding the political causes of Gezi Park Protests

	Participated in Gezi Park Protests	Strongly agree (%)	Agree (%)	Neither agree nor disagree (%)	Disagree (%)	Strongly disagree (%)
Path of the Trees	Yes	6	16	26	36	16
	No	9	0	18	64	9
	Total	7	10	23	47	13
Resist Auntie	Yes	10	10	22	37	21
	No	0	0	9	82	9
	Total	7	7	17	53	16
Occupygezi	Yes	6	11	11	51	21
	No	9	0	9	54	28
	Total	7	7	10	53	23
Pac-Chapull	Yes	11	5	16	32	36
	No	0	0	18	63	19
	Total	7	3	17	43	30
Everyday I'm Chapulling	Yes	11	31	26	16	16
	No	0	9	9	73	9
	Total	7	23	20	37	13

In terms of offering solutions, all the games have been found relatively barren for both the Gezi participants and nonparticipants with up to 76 % (*Occupygezi*) disagreement rates in total for individual games (see Table 5.5). This specific case is interesting since *Occupygezi* was a game proposing a solution to the clashes in the early days of the protest, namely, the nonintervention of the police. But this proposal seems to have lost its relevance for the players. The only different example with relatively higher agreement rates, 42 %, among Gezi Protests participants was *Everyday I'm Chapuling*. The game had different endings portraying different political outcomes depending on the community-building efforts of the players. The players' feeling of agency through the game mechanics could be the reason of this perception. Yet the game had also high disagreement rates among players who did not participate in the protests, 82 %. This difference is noteworthy since it shows a quite different position toward the idea of civic engagement.

There were only few agreements among players regarding the success of individual games in exposing causes, showing new perspectives, and offering solution. Nevertheless, we asked them if the design elements, the rules and the visuals, were effective in regard to convey the political positions of the game (see Table 5.6). In all the games, rules received higher agreement rates between 57 and 70 %. Although they may not have been perceived successful all the time, the designers' efforts to create meaningful interactions seem to be noticed by the players. *Resist Auntie, Pac-Chapull*, and *Everyday I'm Chapulling* also received relatively higher agreement rates between 30 % and 40 % regarding their graphics.

Next we asked players questions regarding their possible future use or interaction with videogames as a form of political discussion. Asked if they would suggest individual games to other players as part of a political commentary, more than half

Table 5.6 The design element was effective in regard to convey the political positions of the game

	Design element	Strongly agree (%)	Agree (%)	Neither agree nor disagree (%)	Disagree (%)	Strongly disagree (%)
Path of the Trees	Graphics	0	14	33	40	13
	Rules	27	44	23	3	3
Resist Auntie	Graphics	10	30	40	13	7
	Rules	17	40	27	13	3
Occupygezi	Graphics	7	3	40	30	20
	Rules	33	27	27	3	10
Pac-Chapull	Graphics	7	24	33	23	13
	Rules	17	47	23	10	3
Everyday I'm Chapulling	Graphics	0	37	33	23	7
	Rules	30	33	20	10	7

Table 5.7 I would suggest the game as part of a political commentary

	Strongly agree (%)	Agree (%)	Neither agree nor disagree (%)	Disagree (%)	Strongly disagree (%)
Path of the Trees	7	37	17	30	9
Resist Auntie	17	37	20	17	10
Occupygezi	20	27	23	20	9
Pac-Chapull	13	23	37	17	10
Everyday I'm Chapulling	30	33	14	23	0

of the players answered positively regarding *Resist Auntie* and *Everyday I'm Chapulling*; with 54 and 63 % agreement rates, respectively (see Table 5.7). Moreover, despite their negative evaluation in some areas listed above; the agreement rate was above 36 % for each individual game.

Our last question was whether or not after playing these games they would consider designing a videogame as part of political protests if they had the skills. 77 % of the players answered positively to this question, while the percentage of players who had created some type of digital content to support the Gezi Protests was 86 %. We might argue that being familiarized to the idea of videogames as a form of civic engagement had encouraged them to use them so.

5.3 Conclusion

Videogames produced during Gezi Park Protests reflect the views of their designers on an ongoing protest against government policies. They were not only encouraging but were used as a form of civic engagement. While some were developed by individuals, others were produced as part of a collective effort which resembles the formation of a forum videogames. The fact that they were produced without the guidance of parent organization such as a political party or a media outlet resembled the practice of citizen journalism. They were independent activist videogames in terms of their political position, supporting a protest; but their short production circle and direct connection to an ongoing event also resembled newsgames or current event games. They didn't have the planning and discussion circle an ideal activist videogame would have in order to form a well-built political argument. Instead, they were taking reactionary positions developed within temporal, logistical, and technical restrictions. While there were repeating themes, each game differed from others in its focus and commentary. Some focused on police violence while others commented on the environmental policies which sparked the protests and so on. This variety continued in their design too. While some borrowed game mechanics from popular arcade and platform games and added imagery related to protests to them, others tried to use game play as an expressive tool.

Our object experiment has shown that the players' participation to Gezi Protests was a key factor in their perception of these games. Players who participated in the protests positioned themselves closer to the opinions expressed in the games or found some issues more relevant such as police violence or civic engagement for political change. These games functioned as historical artifacts representing the Gezi events in varying extents, and the player's own experiences and memories regarding the events created a reference point for contextualizing the games. Even though they were mostly unfamiliar with the use of videogames as forms of political engagement before this experiment, they showed a tendency toward using them as a tool for discussion and even designing future games as a form of civic engagement. Our study was limited with the games currently available online. A future study involving not only other games produced during the Gezi Protests but also a larger test group which reflects the diversities of the protestors and includes participants who objected the protests would provide a much detailed data on the perception of videogames during civic crisis.

References

Allan S (2013) Citizen witnessing: revisioning journalism in times of crisis. Polity, Cambridge

Amnesty International (2013) Gezi Park protests: brutal denial of the right to peaceful assembly in Turkey, Amnesty International. https://www.amnestyusa.org/sites/default/files/eur440222013en.pdf. Accessed 13 Aug 2015

Blumberg FC, Almonte DE, Anthony JS, Hashimoto N (2013) Serious games: what are they? What do they do? Why should we play them? In: Dill K (ed) Oxford handbook of media psychology. Oxford University Press, New York, pp 334–351

Bogost I, Frasca G (2007) Videogames go to Washington: the story behind Howard Dean's videogame propaganda. In: Harrigan P, Wardrip Fruin N (eds) Second person: roleplaying and story in games and playable media. MIT, Cambridge

Bogost I, Ferrari S, Schweizer B (2010) Newsgames: journalism at play. MIT, Cambridge

Clément F (2014) Players/gamers. In: Wolf MJP, Perron B (eds) The Routledge companion to video game studies. Routledge, New York, pp 197–203

Colak E (2014) Art in street: the significant role of using the art, literature and humor in the Gezi resistance. Int J Arts Sci 7(4):463–476, http://universitypublications.net/ijas/0704/pdf/V4NA104.pdf. Accessed 10 Sept 2015

Dagtas S (2013) The politics of humor and humor as politics during Turkey's Gezi Park protests, Fieldsights—hot spots, cultural anthropology online. http://www.culanth.org/fieldsights/397-the-politics-of-humor-and-humor-as-politics-during-turkey-s-gezi-park-protests. Accessed 10 Sept 2015

Ferdig RE (2014) Education. In: Wolf MJP, Perron B (eds) The Routledge companion to video game studies. Routledge, New York, pp 317–323

Flanagan M (2009) Critical play: radical game design. MIT, Cambridge

Frasca G (2004) Videogames of the oppresses: critical thinking, education, tolerance, and other trivial issues. In: Wardrip-Fruin N, Harrigan P (eds) First person: new media as story, performance, and game. MIT, Cambridge, pp 85–94

Game Developers @ Turkey (2013a) Jam#gezi. https://web.archive.org/web/20130614045752/http://gdtjam.com/jamgezi/. Accessed 10 Sept 2015

Game Developers @ Turkey (2013b) Jam#gezi about. https://web.archive.org/web/20130629180222/http://gdtjam.com/jamgezi/. Accessed 10 Sept 2015

Game Developers @ Turkey (2015) #GeziJAM. http://gamedevturkey.com/gezijam/sheet.php?p=gezijam#description. Accessed 10 Sept 2015

Gerbaudo P (2012) Tweets and the streets: social media and contemporary activism. Pluto, London

Global Game Jam (2015) Frequently asked questions. http://globalgamejam.org/faq. Accessed 10 Sept 2015

Gunhan M (2013) Amber Sanat & Teknoloji Festivali'ndeydik! Merlin'in Kazanı 13 November. http://www.merlininkazani.com/. Accessed 10 Sept 2015

ICIDS (2013) The 6th international conference on interactive digital storytelling—exhibition. http://gamesandnarrative.net/icids2013/exhibition. Accessed 06 Sept 2015

Isal A (2013) Gezi Parkı Direnişi Oyunlarla Devam Ediyor. Oyungezer 15 June. http://oyungezer.com.tr/. Accessed 10 Sept 2015

Ive C (2013) Gezi Parkı direnişi oyun oldu: the Çapulcu. Radikal 14 June. http://www.radikal.com.tr/. Accessed 10 Sept 2015

Kahne J, Middaugh E, Evans C (2009) The civic potential of video games. MIT, Cambridge

Kaya C (2013) Diren Teyze. Hurriyet 17 June. http://www.hurriyet.com.tr/. Accessed 10 Sept 2015

Kentel MK (2013) #GEZİJAM. Fareler Oyunda (2):28–35. goo.gl/JgOgmI. Accessed 10 Sept 2015

Koenitz H (2014) Reflecting civic protest—the occupy Istanbul game. Proceedings of the foundations of digital games 2014 conference. http://www.fdg2014.org/papers/fdg2014_poster_06.pdf. Accessed 10 Sept 2015

KONDA (2014) Gezi report: public perception of the 'Gezi protests' who were the people at Gezi Park? http://konda.com.tr/en/raporlar/KONDA_Gezi_Report.pdf. Accessed 13 Aug 2015

Lerner J (2014) Making democracy fun. MIT, Cambridge

Molleindustria (2004) The role of play. http://www.molleindustria.org/node/128/. Accessed 10 Sept 2015

Newsgaming (2003) September 12th, a toy world—political videogame about the war on terror. http://newsgaming.com/press092903.htm. Accessed 10 Sept 2015

Ogun Emre P, Coban B, Sener G, (2014) Humorous form of protest: disproportionate use of intelligence in Gezi Park's resistance. Proceedings of the 13th POLITSCI conference—new opportunities and impasses: theorising and experiencing politics, pp 430–447. http://doc.utwente.nl/92922/1/Politsci13baski-libre.pdf. Accessed 10 Sept 2015

Sicart M (2009) Newsgames: theory and design. In: Stevens SM, Saldamarco SJ (eds) Entertainment computing—ICEC 2008. Springer, Berlin, pp 27–33

Sicart M (2014) Play matters. MIT, Cambridge

Tastan C (2013) The Gezi Park protests in Turkey: a qualitative field research. Insight Turkey 15(3):27–38

Treanor M, Mateas M (2009) Newsgames: procedural rhetoric meets political cartoons. Proceedings of the conference of the digital games research association. http://www.digra.org/wp-content/uploads/digital-library/09300.09505.pdf. Accessed 10 Sept 2015

Varol OO (2014) Revolutionary humor. South Calif Interdiscip Law J 23:555–594, http://ssrn.com/abstract=2325782. Accessed 10 Sept 2015

Ludography

Akay K (2013) Occupygezi. [Online] PC. Self-Published
Alacamli E, Unsal E (2013) Resist Auntie! [Online] PC. Self-Published
Anspach R (1973) Anti-Monopoly. [Board Game] San Francisco: University Games
Aydinoglu D, Aydinoglu N (2013) Direnistan [Online] Facebook MMO. Self-Published
Baby Development Labs (2013) Resist Gezi Park. [Mobile] Mobile. Baby Development Labs
Baysal B, Guller I (2013) Pac-Chapull. [Online] PC. Self-Published
Chapul Games (2013) The Capulcu. [Mobile] Mobile. Chapul Games
Everyday I'm Chapulling (2013) [Online] PC. Self-Published
Global Kids (2008) Ayiti: the cost of life. [Online] PC. New York: Gamelab
Izmo Bilisim (2013) Gezi Parki İsyani. [Online] PC. Oyuncini
Izmo Bilisim (2013) Duran Adam. [Online] PC. Oyuncini
Izmo Bilisim (2013) Marmaray Seysi. [Online] PC. Oyuncini
Kurkcu B (2013) Path of the Trees. [Online] PC. Self-Published
NAMCO (1980) Pac-Man. [Various] Various. Tokyo: Namco Limited
Oyun Dongusu (2013) Capulcu. [Mobile] Mobile. Ankara: Oyun Dongusu
S&T Play (2013) Chapulling. [Mobile] Mobile. Seoul: S&T Play
TAITO (1978) Space Invaders. [Various] Various. Tokyo: Taito Corporation
Temelkuran I, Koenitz H (2013) Occupy Istanbul. [ASAPS] ASAPS. Self-Published

Chapter 6
Psychological Player Profiling with Action Patterns

Barbaros Bostan and Gokhan Sahin

Abstract Profiling aims to deliver personalized content to each player, fitting his or her preferences. Although the aim of profiling and the techniques used for the profiling process vary, the governing idea is to monitor user choices/actions in an environment and compare/process these choices with hypothesized profiles to understand his/her preferences. In this article, our aim is to define patterns (sequence of player actions) that can be matched with player profiles using pattern–motivation pairings. The real-time profiling technique intends to adapt to the psychology of the player by rapidly matching patterns. In this regard, four different types of patterns have been developed for an interactive storytelling project.

Keywords Player profiles • Player types • Pattern matching

6.1 Introduction

Profiling users aims to deliver personalized content to each user, fitting his or her personal interests. Personalization of content and one-to-one marketing has become popular in many popular domains. User profiles represent the emotional and mental states, goals, motivations, decision-making process, and skills of the user. Without knowing anything about the user, any system would perform in exactly the same way for all users. User profiling is used in various contexts, such as identifying travel preferences, designing adaptive teaching and learning programs as well as adaptive e-learning systems, analyzing phone calls, designing intelligent agents, evaluating Internet user preferences based on web browsing data, designing recommender systems such as developing personal assistants that assist to a user with computer-based tasks, supporting employee selection or assessment, etc. Although the aim of profiling and the techniques used for the profiling process vary between these systems, the governing idea is to monitor user choices/actions in an

B. Bostan, Ph.D. (✉) • G. Sahin, Ph.D.
Department of Information Systems and Technologies, Yeditepe University, Istanbul, Turkey
e-mail: bbostan@yeditepe.edu.tr; sahin@yeditepe.edu.tr

© Springer International Publishing Switzerland 2016
B. Bostan (ed.), *Gamer Psychology and Behavior*, International Series
on Computer Entertainment and Media Technology,
DOI 10.1007/978-3-319-29904-4_6

89

environment and compare/process these choices with hypothesized profiles to understand his/her preferences.

User profiling is also a popular research area in computer gaming but it is especially important for interactive storytelling (IS) systems. Since IS systems aim to deliver an individualized response to player actions and choices, user models are applied to provide the system with the ability to tailor the game depending on player preferences. IS systems usually include a "Drama Manager" and a "User Model." The drama manager is responsible for searching and executing sequences of story plots (Bates 1992; Kelso et al. 1993); sequencing story beats based on declarative knowledge (Mateas 1997, 2000; Mateas and Stern 2001); generating stories according to the interaction between virtual actors with dramatic goals and the user (Cavazza et al. 2002); selecting, specifying, and refining story events (Thue et al. 2007); selecting story beats based on a user model (El-Nasr 2007); connecting dilemmas as points of interaction within a coherent plotline (Barber and Kudenko 2008); partial ordering of abstract plot points (Magerko 2005); ranking actions of characters from the most valuable to the least valuable (Szilas 2003). The module or the component that keeps track of user interactions or choices is the User Model or the Player Profiler. The majority of the IS systems focus on the role of the Drama Manager, but all the aforementioned story modifications are dependent on how the system defines player profiles and how it keeps track of user actions while he/she is playing the game.

There is also a great diversity on the techniques used for player profiling and the profiles used for the profiling process. In this regard, researchers usually rely on play styles or player types defined by previous studies. Bartle (2004) identified the famous four play styles as: socializers, achievers, killers, and explorers. Salen and Zimmerman (2003) defined five player types: the standard player, the dedicated player, the unsportsmanlike player, the cheat, and the spoil-sport. Mulligan and Patrovsky (2003) introduced a grouping based on the relations between players: general players, barbarians, tribesman, and citizens; Pohjola (2004), in the context of live-action role-playing defined four categories: immersionist, dramatist, gamist, and simulationist; Dena (2008) defined the three tiers of hardcore gamers as: puzzle players, story players, and real-world players. In terms of player profiling, even the popular playstyles of Bartle (2004) have never been empirically tested to validate that the four player types (Explorers, Achievers, Killers, and Socializers) are independent of each other. If the profile definitions are overlapping, it is very difficult to discriminate between player actions. For example, if the player is killing all the enemies in a computer game, he/she is assumed to be a Killer but his/her motivation could be to collect all items dropped by enemies, to gain all the trophies of the game, to visit every destination in the game by eliminating obstacles, or all of them.

The aforementioned player types are general computer gamer categories which are not specially developed for player profiling process but researchers are also developing their own profiling techniques for IS systems. In example, PASSAGE uses the player types of Peinado and Gervás (2007): fighters, power gamers, tacticians, storytellers, and method actors (Thue et al. 2007); IDA uses an internal probabilistic rule-based model (Magerko 2005); and Mirage uses personality traits

that define a character stereotype (El-Nasr 2007). What IDA focuses with a probabilistic rule-based model is the likelihood of the player violating the preconditions
of story events; it does not use the model explicitly for profiling the player. Mirage
uses personality traits like reluctant hero, violent, self-interested, coward, truth-
seeker, etc. but El-Nasr (2007) also commented that this model is overly simplistic.
In this regard, this article focuses on player motivations like power, affiliation,
aggression, etc. to profile a player. Motivations are more suitable for analyzing a
user's intentions or goals because game playing is a goal-directed behavior and the
attainment of goals or disengagement from unattainable goals are facilitated by
player motivations (Heckhausen and Heckhausen 2005). Motivation can also be
elicited by reward samples (priming) and reward cues (Berridge 2001) to provide an
optimized gaming experience to different types of players.

Customization of the gaming experience requires constant monitoring of the
player actions within the virtual world and different techniques are used to process
this action information into a player profile. PASSAGE learns a player model
expressed as weights for five styles of players; potential courses of action are identified before runtime and augmented with weight deltas (Thue et al. 2007). Whenever
an action is received from the game world, an addition or subtraction is made to the
profile by using the weight value. Mirage use a rule-based system that calculates a
new value for each personality trait vector based on story context, user action, and
previous vector values. The system uses very simple rules, such as "if user advances
to attack unarmed characters, then advance user on the violence scale" (El-Nasr
2007). But these techniques may not be sufficient for the profiling process since
they assume that every single action makes a contribution to player profiling. Every
action does not have to change the profile because player actions may show very
complex patterns in a computer game. For example, the player may kill the monsters to loot their gold and then use them to buy a golden necklace for the princess
to win her heart. If single actions are used for the profiling process, this system may
conclude that this player likes fighting and killing, but his/her true motivation is
later understood. Thus, motivation to reach a goal may be determined by a player's
current action, but it is also dependent on his/her previous and future actions.

There are also different profiling techniques used in contexts other than IS. For
detecting fraud cell phone calls, massive numbers of cellular calls are analyzed with
a data mining approach to determine general patterns of fraud usage and these patterns are processed with a set of rules and a set of templates to profile customers
(Fawcett and Provost 1996). But the amount of data to be processed in profiling
game players is not huge enough to employ data mining techniques on it. Another
technique employed to find user preferences, likes, and dislikes is collaborative filtering (Lashkari et al. 1994). This technique compares data from one user with other
users to find overlaps within interests and if such overlaps exist, the user is recommended new items from the data of other users. In this regard, user profiling in
computer games is not interested in a comparison between users but focuses on each
player as a unique data source. Case Base Reasoning (CBR) is another method of
modeling users. In CBR, the system remembers a history of situations similar to the
current one and uses this information to solve new problems. Thus, profiles are

identified by reference to nearby examples in the problem space. For example, The Personal Travel Assistant of Waszkiewicz et al. (1999) stores user actions when planning a trip in cases and CBR is used to match user actions into profiles.

More complex solutions to user profiling include techniques like Bayesian reasoning or Bayesian Networks which classify items of interest by probabilistic distributions and make optimal decisions by reasoning about these probabilities. There are even hybrid techniques that build user profiles by integrating CBR and Bayesian Networks (Schiaffino and Amandi 2000). Adaptive teaching and learning programs store the data in the form of attribute-value pairs which constitute a user profile and these pairs represent the user's current state of knowledge and personal characteristics, features, preferences, and so forth (Nebel et al. 2003). In intelligent tutoring systems, the domain of teaching is usually well analyzed and structured but the game domain is less structured, and the range and type of player behaviors to track are less predictable than the case of tutoring systems (Beal et al. 2002). Two common techniques employed in user profiling on the Internet are knowledge-based profiling and behavior-based profiling. Knowledge-based models often use questionnaires and interviews to obtain user data and then employ static models of users and match users to the closest model. Behavior-based approaches use the user's behavior as a model, commonly using machine-learning techniques to discover useful patterns in the behavior, but CBR is also employed (Bradley et al. 2000) to profile web users.

6.2   Purpose of Research

Profiling gamers is a real-time task; thus, the aforementioned knowledge-based systems are not suitable because they rely on user data that are obtained before the process to be analyzed. The domain of user profiles in computer games is not complex or big enough to require machine-learning techniques or CBR. To solve the problem of action-contribution pairing for profiling, we use patterns to describe the player's intentions and desires, where a pattern is a sequence of player actions that satisfy a certain motivation. User profiling is thus limited by the requirement that all possible patterns have to be specified before. But if the domain is small enough in which the player can only satisfy a limited number of profiles, this is not a problem. Acquisition of information is implicit and is based on observing actions of the player during the gaming process.

Player behavior may exhibit very complex patterns in the game world where simple play styles may not be sufficient. For example, Player A may wear an expensive trendy suit because he/she does not wish to make a bad impression (Infavoidance) and instead wishes to win B's friendship (Affiliation) so that he/she will learn the secret location (Cognizance) of the celestial map and use the map for finding the lost city of Atlantis (Acquisition) to unlock the secrets of the Mother Civilization (Understanding) and thus level up (Achievement). In this sense, the play styles defined in the literature are very limited: for example, if the player is exploring the whole virtual world, according to Bartle (2004), he/she is assumed to be an Explorer. But his/her motivation could be just to complete all the quests (Achievement), to acquire all unique items (Acquisition), to eliminate every single enemy (Aggression) or could be all of them. Thus, a player model that takes into account motivations, underlying processes, personality traits, general behavior patterns, and correspond-ing individual actions may yield better results in grouping player preferences.

Beyond play styles and gamer types, profiling the player based on his/her needs or motivations is still a theoretical concept which cannot be found in commercial video games, but in research prototypes. There have been attempts to define the underlying motives of players but even the major studies in this area (Malone and Lepper 1987; Sweetser and Wyeth 2005; Yee 2006) cannot reach to an agreement on common motivational variables. In an attempt to define a broader range of moti-vational variables based on formal theories of human motivation, Bostan (2009) proposed a motivational framework based on the psychological needs of Murray (1938) that analyzes player needs in relation to the gaming situations of a role play-ing game (RPG), defines motivation as a product of continuous interactions between players and the virtual world, and describes each individual psychological need in terms of the actions it provokes. Our profiler also uses the 27 motivational variables analyzed by Bostan (2009).

Regarding the need framework of Murray (1938), the following questions have already been answered: (1) the study is still applicable since it defines the basic desires and analyzes the multifaceted nature of intrinsic motivation (Reiss 2004), (2) the study is applicable to motivational studies in interactive/new media such as Facebook (Ines and Abdelkader 2011), (3) the study is suitable for gaming, the needs of the framework have already been investigated in relation to various gam-ing situations that can be experienced in digital RPGs (Bostan 2009), (4) the frame-work is capable of identifying the relationship between psychological needs and game mechanics (Bostan and Kaplancali 2009), (5) the framework is capable of analyzing user-created content (mods) of a computer game in terms of the needs they satisfy (Bostan and Kaplancali 2010), (6) the framework can predict goal-directed behavior of both player and non-player characters in a computer game and can be used to design virtual agents with personality (Bostan 2010), and (7) the framework is suitable for customizing the gaming experience in an IS system (Bostan and Marsh 2012).

6.3 Player Profiler

In an actual IS system, the game world is constantly monitored and player actions are received by the Player Profiler to build player profiles. But since our profiler has not been integrated with an actual game, an Events Class is used to simulate the Game World. The task of this class is to continuously stream player actions to the Profiler. The class has only one method, *ReadEvents* which reads a list of events from a text file and then stores this information in one-dimensional vectors.

These events will later be sent one by one to the Player Profiler, imitating the Game World. We define patterns with an event structure. Every event in the game world consists of a subject (*subjectID*), a location (*locationID*), a verb (*verbID*), one object (*objectID*), and a target (*targetID*) such as "Frodo" at "Shire" village "attacks" with a "sword" to a "villager." Events also have time values indicating the time of the event. Thus, a 1.21.3.7.4,11 corresponds to Event with a *subjectID* of 1, a *locationID* of 21, a *verbID* of 3, an *objectID* of 7, and a *targetID* of 4 that occurs at 11th second. This information is stored in six vectors of the Events Class: vector<int> subjectIDEF, vector<int> locationIDEF, vector<int> verbIDEF, vector<int>objectIDEF, vector<int> targetIDEF, vector<int> eventTimeEF.

6.3.1 Profiler Pattern Descriptions

Every pattern has a unique id and patterns consist of a number of events which are specified with an *eventID*. For example, if Frodo has a *subjectID* of 1, the village of Shire has a *locationID* of 21, attack has a *verbID* of 3, and object "sword" and target "villager" are identified with IDs of 7 and 4, then a 1.21.3.7.4 is the unique *eventID* for this specific event. We use a flag structure to define the nature of events that define the sequence. For example, events can be continuous in nature, which means that they have a strict sequence where an event is immediately followed by another. Or patterns can be identified with more fluid structures, such as those where other events can be placed between the two events of the sequence. All these variations are represented with flags. For example, a flag of 1 means exact match and a flag of −1 means NOT (this event should not be in the event sequence) (Table 6.1).

An example pattern is: 2,1,1.21.3.7.4,1,1.21.4.0.4,−2. These are: 2(*PatternID*), 1(*Flag1*), 1(*SubjectID1*), 21(*LocationID1*), 3(*VerbID1*), 7(*ObjectID1*), 4(*TargetID1*), 1(*Flag2*), 1(*SubjectID2*), 21(*LocationID2*), 4(*VerbID2*), 0(*ObjectID2*), 4(*TargetID2*), −2(*End of Pattern*). So, this pattern has an ID of 2, the first event to be received is a 3.7.4 by 1 at location 21 with a flag of 1, the next event to be received is also a 4.0.4 by 1 at 21 with a flag of 1. Flags determine the structure and the definition of each pattern. In this example, if the user is attacking a "villager" with a "sword," we can assume that the player is aggressive enough to attack weaponless villagers. But in the next dialogue option, he apologizes the villager with a *verbID* of 4 for apologize, an *objectID* of 0 (no object) and a *targetID* of 4. Now we understand that the player has accidentally attacked the villager and he/she proved it by apologizing, so the attack cannot be classified as an indicator of aggression. All these pattern definitions, which have been stored in a data file, are transferred to a two-dimensional vector. So, with two indexes, any information can be retrieved from this vector.

Table 6.1 General pattern structure

PatternID	Flag	EventID	Flag	EventID	...	End flag

6.3.1.1   Continuous Patterns

Continuous patterns are those that require events immediately followed by other events. An example is key presses of a game player to activate a combo sequence. For example, an X press, immediately followed by a Y press which is immediately followed by a Z press, may be a combo sequence that we are watching from the game world (Table 6.2).

Pattern number 4's last event is a 1.7.4.0.0 (Dante at Purgatory presses z button) with a flag of 1 (direct match), event before the last one is a 1.7.3.0.0 (Dante at Purgatory presses y button) with a flag of 1 and the first event is 1.7.2.0.0 (Dante at Purgatory presses x button) with a flag of 1. So, the algorithm is now searching the action list for patterns that end with a 1.7.4.0.0; if there is any, then looks for a 1.7.3.0.0; if it finds any, it looks for a 1.7.2.0.0. The final −2 is the end of flag statement.

6.3.1.2   Continuous Patterns with NOT

Continuous patterns are those that require events that are NOT immediately followed by other events. An example is key presses of a game player to activate a combo sequence. For example, an X press, NOT followed by a Y press, which is immediately followed by a Z press, may be a combo sequence that we are watching from the game world (Table 6.3).

Pattern number 5's last event is a 1.7.4.0.0 (Dante at Purgatory presses z button) with a flag of 1 (direct match), event before the last one is NOT a 1.7.3.0.0 (Dante at Purgatory presses y button) with a flag of −1 and the first event is 1.7.2.0.0 (Dante at Purgatory presses X button) with a flag of 1. So, the algorithm is now searching the action list for patterns that end with a 1.7.4.0.0; if there is any, then looks for anything but a 1.7.3.0.0; if it matches the condition, it looks for a 1.7.2.0.0. The final −2 is the end of flag statement.

6.3.1.3   Discontinuous Patterns with Last Match

These patterns are non-continuous, actions does not have to follow other actions immediately. Also, it looks for the nearest match in the action sequence. All the previous matches are not considered. An example is the statistics of a football

Table 6.2 Continuous patterns

4	1	1.7.2.0.0	1	1.7.3.0.0	1	1.7.4.0.0	−2

Table 6.3 Continuous patterns with NOT

5	1	1.7.2.0.0	−1	1.7.3.0.0	1	1.7.4.0.0	−2

game which are continuously monitored to understand player profiles. For example, we might be looking for corner kicks that end with the scoring of a goal in order to find whose corner kicks or shots are more effective. In this pattern, there can be many events between the corner kick and the goal, like "Ronaldo shoots," "Bravo saves the shoot," "Iniesta fouls Benzema," etc. But we are not interested in what happens between the corner kick and the goal, we are interested in a sequence that ends with a goal, that has ANY action in between, and that starts with a corner kick (Table 6.4).

The pattern begins with any player (0) at Bernabéu Stadium (9) uses a corner kick (2) and ends with any player (0) at Bernabéu Stadium (9) scores a goal (4). Between these two events anything (0.0.0.0.0) can happen (match any event flag of 2). So, the algorithm is now searching the action list for patterns that end with a 0.9.4.0.0, if there is any, then looks for anything and ignores anything as long as it founds a 0.9.2.0.0 at the end. The final −2 is the end of flag statement. Assume that we have an action sequence as given below (Table 6.5).

When we receive the event 10.9.4.0.0 (goal) from the game world, the algorithm now tries to match patterns that end with a 10.9.4.0.0 such as the pattern 7 given above. For this pattern, it now starts searching through the action sequence. It is now looking for the corner kick event ignoring any other. It finds a corner kick at 14:10 and another corner kick at 14:30. Which one will be used to match the pattern? The last one will be used. "LAST MATCH" definition is given with the flag 2 combined with the *eventID* of 0.0.0.0.0 in the pattern definition. So, the matched pattern starts at 14:30 and ends at 14:36. These pattern matches can also be limited in time so that it will only match patterns where the *(pattern end—pattern start) < specified length of time*. It is also possible to define minimum length of time (min) and maximum length of time (max) for matching patterns. So, only patterns that satisfy the *min < (pattern end—pattern start) < max* condition will be matched.

Table 6.4 Discontinuous pattern with last match example

7	1	0.9.2.0.0	2	0.0.0.0.0	1	0.9.4.0.0	−2

Table 6.5 Discontinuous pattern with last match example

Subject	Location	Verb	Object	Target	Time	Description
8	9	5	0	11	13:40	Iniesta passes the ball to Neymar
11	9	7	0	0	13:46	Neymar shoots
1	9	11	0	0	13:47	Navar saves
22	9	2	0	0	14:10	Alves uses a corner kick
10	9	7	0	0	14:13	Messi shoots
4	9	10	0	0	14:14	Ramos clears the ball for a corner
22	9	2	0	0	14:30	Alves uses a corner kick
11	9	5	0	10	14:34	Neymar passes the ball to Messi
10	9	4	0	0	14:36	Messi scores a goal

6.3.1.4   Discontinuous Patterns with Last Match & NOT

These patterns are noncontinuous and actions does not have to follow other actions immediately. Also, it looks for the nearest match in the action sequence. All the previous matches are not considered. An example is the statistics of a football game which are continuously monitored to understand player profiles. For example, we might be looking for corner kicks that end with the scoring of a goal in order to find whose corner kicks or shots are more effective. In this pattern, there can be many events between the corner kick and the goal, like "Ronaldo shoots," "Bravo saves the shoot," "Iniesta fouls Benzema," "Referee flags an offside," etc. But we are not interested in what happens between the corner kick and the goal, as long as we do NOT have a "referee flags an offside"; we are interested in a sequence that ends with a goal, that has ANY action in between, and that starts with a corner kick (Table 6.6).

The pattern begins with any player (0) at Bernabéu Stadium (9) uses a cornerkick (2) and ends with any player (0) at Bernabéu Stadium (9) scores a goal (4). Between these two events, anything can happen and the only exception is the "referee (8) at Bernabéu Stadium (9) flags on offside (3)." So, the algorithm is now searching for pattern definitions that end with a 0.9.4.0.0; if there is any, then looks for anything and ignores anything but the 8.9.3.0.0 as long as it founds a 0.9.2.0.0 at the end. The final −2 is the end of flag statement. Assume that we have an action sequence as given below (Table 6.7).

When we receive the event 10.9.4.0.0 (goal) from the game world, the algorithm now tries to match patterns that end with a 10.9.4.0.0 such as the pattern 8 given above. For this pattern, it now starts searching through the action sequence. It is now looking for the corner kick event ignoring any event other than an offside. It finds a corner kick at 14:10 and another corner kick at 14:30. The algorithm uses the last match but since the referee flags an offside at 14:36 the pattern 8 is not matched.

Table 6.6 Discontinuous patterns with last match & NOT

| 8 | 1 | 0.9.2.0.0 | −3 | 8.9.3.0.0 | 1 | 0.9.4.0.0 | −2 |

Table 6.7 Discontinuous pattern with last match & NOT example

Subject	Location	Verb	Object	Target	Time	Description
8	9	5	0	11	13:40	Iniesta passes the ball to Neymar
11	9	7	0	0	13:46	Neymar shoots
1	9	11	0	0	13:47	Navar saves
22	9	2	0	0	14:10	Alves uses a corner kick
10	9	7	0	0	14:13	Messi shoots
4	9	10	0	0	14:14	Ramos clears the ball for a corner
22	9	2	0	0	14:30	Alves uses a corner kick
11	9	5	0	10	14:34	Neymar passes the ball to Messi
99	9	3	0	0	14:36	Referee flags an offside
10	9	4	0	0	14:36	Messi scores a goal

6.3.2 Profiler Structure and Processing Patterns

The Profiler Class is responsible for reading the defined action patterns and it uses the stored information (PatternData.dat) to match patterns. It is also responsible for reading the contribution of each pattern from a file (Contribution.dat) and reading Motivation Names from another file (MotName.dat). There are patterns to be matched but each pattern makes a contribution to a motivational variable in our system. The Pattern file gives only the ID and description of the pattern. But how much contribution every pattern makes is stored in the Contributions file. The format of this file is: 1-2-1, the first variable is Pattern ID, the next variable is Motivation ID, and the final one is the contribution. So, we know that Pattern 1 makes a +1 contribution to Motivation 2. But we do not know Motivation 2's name for displaying output on the screen. This information is stored in the Motivation Names file, which has the following format: 0 Affiliation. The first variable is the Motivation ID and the next one is Motivation Name. So, in the initial phase, all these files are read by the Profiler Class. Later, patterns will be processed and once the patterns are processed, matching pattern information will ideally be sent to an Experience Manager or a Drama Manager but as for now this information is stored in another text file (Planning.txt) in order to simulate this process. The stored information contains both the latest contribution to motivational variables (such as "Affiliation Motivation increased by 2") and the updated total of the motivational variable that increased or decreased (such as "Current Affiliation level is 8").

Assume that we are developing an IS game that focuses on children using two motivational variables: aggression and affiliation. Aggression motivation is related with the following actions: to attack or injure; to murder; to belittle, harm, or maliciously ridicule a person. Affiliation motivation is related to the following actions: to form friendships and associations; to greet, join, and live with others; to cooperate and converse sociably with others; to love; to join groups. It should be noted that almost every commercial computer game requires the player to kill their opponents. There may be some dialogue options to negotiate or barter or intimidate but in the end the player has to attack or harm some enemies. The game will incorporate gaming choices that give the player a chance to choose love or friendship instead of aggression. The children playing the game will have a sword and magic brush to overcome obstacles. The sword will be the aggressive solution and the magic brush will neutralize enemies and allow the player to befriend them. The player analyzer will constantly monitor player actions and profile the children in order to understand if they are inclined toward aggression or affiliation, in a broader sense of view war or peace.

So, as the child plays the game, a sequence of actions will be delivered to the player profiler. If the child attacks a nonaggressive NPC such as a villager, this action contributes to aggression motivation with a modifier of +5. If the child attacks an enemy, this action contributes to aggression motivation with a modifier of +1. If the child uses the magic brush to paint an enemy with love, this action will contribute to affiliation motivation with a modifier of +1. If the child meets an enemy and initiates a dialogue option to persuade him/her to choose love instead of violence, this action will contribute to affiliation motivation with a modifier of +5. There may be many different patterns such as accidentally pressing the attack button and then initiating a dialogue option that ends the encounter well or initiating a dialogue option first but then deciding to kill the enemy that ends the encounter badly.

Thus, whenever a new action is received from the game world, the player profiler will consult the pattern definitions and look for a pattern that ends with the received action. If it finds matches, it will search the action history based on the pattern definitions to match the patterns and to make a motivation contribution toward profiling the child. The profiling information will then be passed to the drama manager. The drama manager will be responsible for customizing the virtual world based on player choices. If the player is an aggressor, it will transform the 3D world, the objects, and the props within it so that the world will look more hideous, gloomier. The models will be more frightening with physical transformations; the colors and the brightness value for models will be changed. If the player chooses peace over aggression, the world will have more vibrant colors, the models will have more lighting, and the world will look more appealing to the eye.

Drama manager will also introduce non-player characters into the world based on the player's profile. There will be two mentor characters in the game that gives advice to the children, one will emphasize the importance of love and affection, and the other will goad the player to more aggressive solutions. The gaming rewards will also be customized based on the profile. If the player is oriented toward aggression, more powerful swords will be introduced and if the player is oriented toward affiliation, the magical brush will gain additional powers that will help the player to solve the problems. The drama manager will also change the story based on the player actions. Every attack or every enemy killed will cause more problems within the virtual world. Every friendship or every neutralized enemy will help the player to solve a problem that threatens the world. The drama manager will provide ethical choices to teach the children what is good and what is bad, what is best for the world, and what is worst. The good mentor may use quotations from religious or spiritual sources and the main theme of the game is that: violence is not a solution. "An eye for an eye will only make the whole world blind."—Mahatma Gandhi.

6.4 Conclusion

The profiling techniques used in other contexts may not be suitable for analyzing computer games. For example, data mining for players requires information about the player to be stored in a database which will then be questioned with queries but real-time data mining will not be fast enough and will require more processing power, thus affecting the performance of the computer game. Comparing player information will also require a server for storing the database and players with slow

Fig. 6.1 Player profiler in an interactive storytelling system

Internet connections or low-performance computers will face other problems. Player actions are dependent on the computer game played and there is not a universal domain that defines all the possible player actions, so Case-Based Reasoning or Bayesian Networks may not suit well to rapidly profile players. The goal of our system is to design a fast and effective Player Profiler between the Game World and the Drama Manager that will help the system customize the gaming experience for each player (Fig. 6.1).

Since there is a great diversity on the techniques used for player profiling and player types in literature are not specially developed for player profiling process, we defined action patterns and matched each pattern with appropriate player motivations. Game playing is a goal-directed behavior and the attainment of goals or disengagement from unattainable goals is facilitated by player motivations. Every action does not have to change the profile because player actions may show very complex patterns in a computer game and player actions are meaningful as a continuous stream. It should be noted that the player actions before the last player action may affect the meaning of the final action. Assuming that every single player action contributes to an independent profile will be oversimplifying a very complex process.

The majority of the IS systems focuses on the Drama Manager and do not deal with the profiling problems. In this study, we designed a player profiler that is suitable for games with a limited number of actions and that can profile the player in real time by matching actions with patterns, also making motivational contributions toward a profile. The C++ profiler requires low processing power and rapidly profiles the player. The dynamic profiler does not focus on single actions but the history of player actions to inform the Drama Manager of the player profile. The profiling patterns analyzed in this study are Continuous Patterns, Continuous Patterns with NOT, Discontinuous Patterns with Last Match, and Discontinuous Patterns with Last Match & NOT. These four simple pattern structures are suitable for analyzing games with a limited set of player actions and the motivational variables used in this study can easily be matched with motivations since Murray (1938) defined actions suitable for each motivational variable in his study.

References

Barber H, Kudenko D (2008) Generation of Dilemma-based interactive narratives with a changeable story goal. In: Proceedings of second international conference on intelligent technologies for interactive entertainment (INTETAIN)

Bartle RA (2004) Designing virtual worlds. New Riders, Indianapolis

Bates J (1992) Virtual reality, art, and entertainment. Presence 1(1):133–138

Beal CR, Beck J, Westbrook D, Atkin M, Cohen P (2002) Intelligent modeling of the user in interactive entertainment. In: Proceedings of the AAAI spring symposium

Berridge KC (2001) Reward learning: reinforcement, incentives and expectations. In: Medin DL (ed) Psychology of learning and motivation, vol 40., pp 223–278

Bostan B (2009) Player motivations: a psychological perspective. ACM Comput Entertain 7(2). http://dl.acm.org/citation.cfm?doid=1541895.1541902

Bostan B (2010) A motivational framework for analyzing player and virtual agent behavior. Entertain Comput 1(3–4):139–146. doi:10.1016/j.entcom.2010.09.002

Bostan B, Kaplancali U (2009) Explorations in player motivations: game mechanics. In: Proceedings of GAMEON 2009, Düsseldorf, Germany

Bostan B, Kaplancali U (2010) Explorations in player motivations: game mods. In: Proceedings of GAMEON-ASIA 2010, Shanghai, China

Bostan B, Marsh T (2012) Fundamentals of interactive storytelling. Acad J Inform Technol 3(8):19–42, www.ajit-e.org/download_pdf.php?id=46&f=46_rev1.pdf&gt

Bradley K, Rafter R, Smyth B (2000) Case-based user profiling for content personalisation. In: International conference on adaptive hypermedia and adaptive web-based systems (AH2000)

Cavazza M, Charles F, Mead SJ (2002) Interacting with virtual characters in interactive storytelling. In: Proceedings of the first ACM joint conference on autonomous agents and multiagent systems, Bologna, Italy, pp 318–325

Dena C (2008) Emerging participatory culture practices: player-created tiers in alternate reality games. Convergence 14:41–57

El-Nasr MS (2007) Interaction, narrative, and drama creating an adaptive interactive narrative using performance arts theories. Interact Stud 8(2):209–240

Fawcett T, Provost F (1996) Combining data mining and machine learning for effective user profiling. In: Proceedings of the 2nd International conference on knowledge discovery and data mining

Heckhausen J, Heckhausen H (2005) Motivation and action. Cambridge University Press, Cambridge

Ines DL, Abdelkader G (2011) Facebook games: between social and personal aspects. Int J Comp Inform Syst Ind Manage Appl 3:713–723

Kelso M, Weyhrauch P, Bates J (1993) Dramatic presence. Presence 2(1):1–15

Lashkari Y, Metral M, Maes P (1994) Collaborative interface agents. In: Proceedings of the Twelfth national conference on artificial intelligence

Magerko B (2005) Story representation and interactive drama. In: Proceedings of the 1st conference on artificial intelligence and interactive digital entertainment

Malone TW, Lepper MR (1987) Making learning fun: a taxonomy of intrinsic motivations for learning. In: Snow RE, Farr MJ (eds) Conative and affective process analyses. Lawrence Erlbaum, Hillsdale

Mateas M (1997) An Oz-centric review of interactive drama and believable agents. In: AI today: recent trends and developments. Lecture notes in artificial intelligence, vol 1600. pp 297–328

Mateas M (2000) A neo-Aristotelian theory of interactive drama. In: Proceedings of AAAI spring symposium on AI and interactive entertainment

Mateas M, Stern A (2001) Interactive drama. A Thesis Proposal', Ph.D. Thesis, Carnegie Mellon University, Pittsburgh

Mulligan J, Patrovsky B (2003) Developing online games. An insider's guide. New Riders, Indianapolis

Murray HA (1938) Explorations in personality. Oxford University Press, New York

Nebel I, Smith B, Paschke R (2003) A user profiling component with the aid of user ontologies. In: Workshop learning—teaching—knowledge—adaptivity (LLWA 03), Karlsruhe

Peinado F, Gervás P (2007) Automatic direction of automatic storytelling: formalizing the game master paradigm. In: Proceedings of the 4th international conference on virtual storytelling: using virtual reality technologies for storytelling (ICVS)

Pohjola M (2004) Autonomous identities: immersion as a tool for exploring, empowering and emancipating identities. In: Montola M, Stenros J (eds) Beyond role and play: tools, toys and theory for harnessing the imagination. Ropecon Ry, Helsinki, pp 81–96

Reiss S (2004) Multifaceted nature of intrinsic motivation: the theory of 16 basic desires. Rev Gen Psychol 8(3):179–193

Salen K, Zimmerman E (2003) Rules of play: game design fundamentals. MIT, Cambridge

Schiaffino SN, Amandi A (2000) User profiling with case-based reasoning and Bayesian networks. In: IBERAMIA-SBIA 2000 open discussion track, pp 12–21

Sweetser P, Wyeth P (2005) GameFlow: a model for evaluating player enjoyment in games. ACM Comput Entertain 3(3). http://dl.acm.org/citation.cfm?doid=1077246.1077253

Szilas N (2003) IDTension: a narrative engine for interactive drama. In: Proceedings of the technologies for interactive digital storytelling and entertainment (TIDSE) conference, pp 187–203

Thue D, Bulitko V, Spetch M, Wasylishen E (2007) Interactive storytelling: a player modelling approach. In: Proceedings of artificial intelligence and interactive digital entertainment conference (AIIDE), Stanford, California, pp 43–48

Waszkiewicz P, Cunningham P, Byrne C (1999) Case-based user profiling in a personal travel assistant. In: User modeling: proceedings of the 7th international conference, pp 323–325

Yee N (2006) Motivations of play in online games. Cyberpsychol Behav 9(6):772–775

Part III
Player Psychology and Motivations

Chapter 7
Game Design and Gamer Psychology

Barbaros Bostan and Ozhan Tingoy

Abstract Gaming is often criticized as being a mindless addiction, but playing a computer game is not a mindless act. Games require complex and different talents such as focusing on a virtual world, thinking as a different person, making strategies, planning, and most importantly interacting with the virtual. Players become the hero of a computer game, try to act, think, and react like him/her. Players have a complicated psychology and to understand computer games, first we need to understand the psychological components specific for this communication medium. It is also important to understand what is fun, what motivates or entertains the player. It is impossible to design a game that pleases the player without understanding the gamer psychology. In this regard, we selected *The Witcher 3: Wild Hunt* game for analyzing gamer psychology under five sections: Realism/Believability, Complexity/Playability, Satisfaction/Fun, Presence/Immersion, and Freedom/Choice.

Keywords Player psychology • Realism • Believability • Playability • Fun • Presence • Immersion • Freedom of choice

7.1 Introduction

Time's "man of the year" for 1982 was "the computer" and the person that excitedly waited for his name to appear on the magazine was Steve Jobs. On January 18, 1982, Time magazine also acknowledged the impact of the video game industry with a cover that declares, "Video Games Are Blitzing the World." The article identified computer games as the prominent feature of the computer revolution, stating that 20 different companies were selling $2 million worth of computer

B. Bostan, Ph.D. (✉)
Department of Information Systems and Technologies, Yeditepe University,
Istanbul, Turkey
e-mail: bbostan@yeditepe.edu.tr

O. Tingoy, Ph.D.
Department of Information Systems, Marmara University, Istanbul, Turkey
e-mail: otingoy@marmara.edu.tr

© Springer International Publishing Switzerland 2016
B. Bostan (ed.), *Gamer Psychology and Behavior*, International Series
on Computer Entertainment and Media Technology,
DOI 10.1007/978-3-319-29904-4_7

games annually and predicts that half of the personal computers are dedicated to computer games. In the present day, computers are a must-have in our lives and digital games are one of the most popular computer applications. Today, World of Warcraft has 10 million active players and the Massive Multiplayer Online Games (MMOG) market is forecasted to reach $15 billion. Computer games are no longer an entertainment but also a science discipline. Universities are opening undergraduate and graduate game design programs, and academic journals specialized in computer games are being published.

Game playing is definitely not a passive action like reading a book or watching a movie. The thing that we define as a computer game constitutes choices in our mind, a virtual world that we enter, and a new personality that we transform into. Gaming is often criticized as being a mindless addiction but playing a computer game is not a mindless act. Games require complex and different talents such as focusing on a virtual world, thinking as a different person, making strategies, planning, and most importantly interacting with the virtual. Players become the hero of the computer game, try to act, think and react like him/her. Players have a complicated psychology and to understand computer games, first we need to understand the psychological components specific for this communication medium. Nowadays, users can change the content of a computer game and make additions to it. It is impossible to change the book of a chapter or rewrite the script of a movie but games are offering new opportunities to us. Gamers are designing their own programs or mods that reflect what they desire to see or experience in the game. It is also important to understand what is fun, what motivates or entertains the player. It is impossible to design a game that pleases the player without understanding the gamer psychology.

The selected computer game for analyzing gamer psychology is *The Witcher 3: Wild Hunt* developed by CD Projekt and released in the second quarter of 2015. The game is set in a dark fantasy world inspired by the works of Polish author Andrej Sapkowski and witchers are monster hunters for hire with extraordinary abilities. It is not the game's mechanics or the visual realism of its virtual world that makes it a perfect choice for analyzing gamer psychology, but it is the behavioral realism of its synthetic agents, the maturity of its fantasy world full of social issues and conflicts, and in the freedom it allows players to make complex choices that enable the game to satisfy a wide range of psychological needs. Instead of making good vs. evil choices, players usually find themselves in situations that require choosing between the lesser of two evils. These choices directly affect the virtual environment and govern the player's interactions with the inhabitants of the fantasy world. The game won the Golden Joystick Awards 2015 in the following categories: Best Storytelling, Best Visual Design, Best Gaming Moment, Studio of the Year, Ultimate Game of the Year.[1]

---

[1] 30 October 2015, https://en.wikipedia.org/wiki/Golden_Joystick_Award#2015

7.2   Realism/Believability

Good games do not simulate physical reality; they mirror emotional reality.[2]
Chris Crawford, Game Designer and Writer

Realism is an extension of human perception. When the physical stimuli received from the virtual world are similar to the physical stimuli received from the real world, the perception is more realistic. But the virtual worlds offered by computer games, because of the technological limitations, usually focus on the sense of sight and hearing. Thus, the realism of the virtual environment is defined in terms of the realism of graphics and sounds delivered by a game. Although the console controllers provide some form of force feedback during gameplay, they are still too far away from a realistic tactile experience. More realism can be experienced in 4D movies where the simulated effects include rain, wind, strobe lights, and vibration. Even though it is still a dream, computer games need design models that appeal to the five human senses to provide more realistic experiences (Storms and Zyda 2000).

Twenty five years before, for those that own a Commodore 64 or Amiga system, the computer games of that period were amazing. The graphics may seem very simple today, but the virtual world they represent was realistic then and players still spent hours in front of the screen. The physical or behavioral realism of those games cannot be compared with today's computer games but they were still entertaining. As technology advanced, our expectations from computer games also changed but realism in a computer game can be defined as the degree of resemblance the virtual world, the virtual objects, and the virtual characters have with their real-world counterparts. Today's computer games feature realistic physical light sources that simulate the interaction between light rays and objects, characters that cast shadows as they pass under street lamps, flames that glint off metal swords, but realism also has conceptual and behavioral aspects (Cheng and Cairns 2005).

So, what is conceptual realism? As one of the most anticipated game releases of 2015 after being teased for well over a year, *The Witcher 3: Wild Hunt* delivers amazing graphics that offer virtual realism beyond expectations. But since the game is set in a dark fantasy world inspired by the works of Polish author Andrej Sapkowski and is the third game in the Witcher series, people already have an idea about the world, its inhabitants, its struggles, and atmosphere. Therefore the story, the characters, and the society should conform to the conceptual framework defined in the novels and the previous titles. For example, the players know that the protagonist of the game, Geralt of Rivia, had a romantic relationship with the sorceress Triss Merigold but another sorceress Yennefer of Vengerberg was also indirectly mentioned on several occasions in the previous titles hinting romance. So, when *The Witcher 3: Wild Hunt* starts with a note sent by Yennefer to Geralt of Rivia stating that she needed to meet him urgently, the players already expect some form of romance or even some form of tension between Triss and Yennefer. Romance options have already been defined in the player's mind and they expect the characters within the game to behave in conformity with the conceptual framework developed by the novels and the previous titles (Fig. 7.1).

---

[2] Crawford, C. (2003) Chris Crawford On Game Design. Boston, MA: New Riders, p.31.

Fig. 7.1 Romance with Triss Merigold (with permission of CD Projekt Red)

Behavioral realism is not only about the characters within the virtual world but also related with how objects/characters physically interact with the player. For example, the Aard Sign is a simple magical sign used by witchers comprised of a telekinetic thrust that can stun, repel, knock down, or disarm opponents. So, the players already have an idea about how the objects/characters react to this telekinetic thrust and of course they expect more realism in the way objects react to this power and maybe anticipate improvements to how to use this power as a witcher. In this context, the AI in *The Witcher 3: Wild Hunt* is programmed to keep enemies together during fights and the developers introduced an alternative form of Aard that the player can shape into a 360° sweep that knocks opponents back from multiple angles. This alternative form is perfect for situations where Geralt is surrounded by many opponents, particularly bandits or fast moving monsters, and also conforms to the basic mechanics of Aard introduced in the previous titles. Since objects and enemies are knocked down in a believable way, the behavioral realism of the Aard sign meets the player's expectations, even exceeds them.

Another concept closely related with realism is believability, in other worlds how believable the virtual worlds are for players. In fact, the more believable the virtual world the more realistic it is and vice versa. Believability from a communication perspective is the willingness of the reader, viewer, or the user to ignore the limitations of the communication channel and to accept the transmitted messages as meaningful and real (Laurel 1993). Believability of virtual worlds in literature often comes along with the term "believable agents". These agents are similar to real-world characters so that they have their own motivations, their own personality, and they react to the changes in the virtual world (Mateas 1997). Today's computer games have AI-driven virtual agents with a 24-h schedule, a distinguishing personality, and a prominent voice actor that brings that character to life. The key concept with believability of an agent is his/her personality which is comprised of motivations, emotions, desires, and goals. Believable agents should be aware of the changes in the virtual world surrounding them and should react to player actions. Since the believability of virtual characters also affect the believability of the story, believable agents is one of the most popular and challenging design issues for game developers. Programmed AI actions are not enough for designing believable characters. If the player does not know who the character is, what he/she wants or why he/she is doing a particular action, the believability of the agent may suffer a blow. It should also be noted that virtual characters are not solitary entities but they live in a society so that they have their own worldviews, culture, history, friends, and enemies.

The virtual world of *The Witcher 3: Wild Hunt* can be described with a single word: misery. As war passes over the region, it leaves behind people that are lacking food and comfort, desolate fields infested with monsters, ransacked and empty towns. So, the player has to deal with tragedy at every step, envy between classes and jealousy among individuals often lead to a sad story or misfortune that the protagonist of the story has to deal with. The harsh realities of the world are also genuinely reflected into the personalities of the virtual agents. The player meets many people with shattered hopes or tragic love stories and these characters, even the minor non-player characters (NPCs), are believable because they feel like they belong to this cursed land. Throughout the game, the effects of war on people are perfectly blended with greed, hatred, and love. These virtual agents are not emotionless, aimless, individual AI-driven entities, but smaller and meaningful pieces of a larger picture that depicts the horrors of war (Fig. 7.2).

Besides virtual agents game mechanics should also be believable. For example, combat in *The Witcher 3: Wild Hunt* usually takes place with a silver sword (for monsters) and a steel sword (for humans) but there is also a crossbow that can be used against flying opponents or underwater. When the player uses

Fig. 7.2 Corpses on a battlefield (with permission of CD Projekt Red)

the crossbow underwater, the game mechanics introduce a one-shot-kill opportunity. Any siren or drowner encountered under the water can be killed with a single bolt but when the player encounters the same monsters on land, they are much harder to kill. The designers introduced a game mechanic that will simplify underwater combat but it simply lacks believability. The crossbow is given as an ordinary weapon to the player and the story provided no explanation on why it is so powerful under the water. If it was described as an enchanted crossbow that magically coats every bolt with a deadly poison when used under the water, this may strengthen the believability of the weapon.

Kamal (2003) defined three qualities that explain believability in computer games: agency, consistency, and fidelity. Agency is the satisfying power to take meaningful action and see the results of our decisions and choices. In this regard, *The Witcher 3: Wild Hunt* provides genuine opportunities. Choices in this game are not white and black stereotypes and players usually find themselves in situations that require choosing between the lesser of two evils. The results of choices can either be immediately experienced or later encountered as the story advances. For example, in the city of Novigrad, people were burnt at the stake for witchcraft by the church of the Eternal Fire. If the player helps the mages to escape the city, in the absence of mages the Witch Hunters decide to unleash their wrath on nonhumans instead and start burning dwarves and elves at the stake. The second quality of believability, consistency, is ensuring that given the same state, an action will lead to the same sort of behavior. For example, people usually fear or suspect witchers and think that they are opportunists that rob the good people of their money by solving supernatural problems that cannot be solved by anyone else. The reactions of people throughout the land when they meet a witcher are consistent with these common beliefs. People fear, shun, or scold the player wherever he/she goes. The third quality of believability, fidelity, is defined as the level of realism that a simulation presents as a whole. *The Witcher 3: Wild Hunt* models weather cycles and night/day cycles. This modeling also has determinable effects on the characters of the world. The characters sleep at night, the shops are closed after dark, the number of monsters encountered in the wilderness is doubled at night, and people run for cover when it rains. So the game provides a high degree of realism as a world simulation (Fig. 7.3).

7.3 Complexity/Playability

> In some cases you have to choose between realism and playability. And the main reason people play games is not for a perfect simulation of the real world but for having fun.[3]
> Jörg Beilschmidt, Game Designer

Complexity and playability are two opposing forces in game design. Players should be able to predict how the game will react to his/her actions and complexity should be finely tuned according to the theme of the game. For example, a player's fatigue is minimized by varying activities and pacing during game play and *The Witcher 3: Wild Hunt* introduces fist fights, horse races, and gwent (card game) challenges to

---

[3] http://www.adventure-island.nl/other.php?file=interviews/interviewsecretfilestunguska_eng

Fig. 7.3 Victim burning at the stake in the city of Novigrad (with permission of CD Projekt Red)

relieve and entertain the player but the mechanics are simple and understandable. On the other hand, if you are playing a horse racing or fist fighting game, the mechanics will be complex and it will take time to learn how the game reacts to key presses or mouse clicks. If you are playing a horse racing simulation for jockeys or a fist fighting simulation for boxers, the complexity will increase since it aims to teach you real-world skills. So the complexity of the gaming mechanics is dependent on the user's knowledge and previous experience. A perfect simulation will be realistic and believable but for those that are not experts in that area, it will be very complex. Difficulty levels in computer games also serve the same purpose. People play computer games for fun and for some people it may be too easy but for others it may be too difficult to play the game. So, computer games usually give you the option to select a difficulty level at the very beginning of the game. *The Witcher 3: Wild Hunt* doesn't use the "easy, medium, hard" naming convention but opts for "Just the Story, Story and Sword, Blood and Broken Bones, and Death March" difficulty levels instead.

Computer games also introduce tutorials where the game teaches the player the basics and trains him/her before the real game starts. These techniques reduce the complexity and make the game mechanics understandable even for the inexperienced. After the opening cut scene, Geralt (the protagonist of the game) finds himself in Kaer Morhen, the last remaining stronghold of the Witchers. In this tutorial, the player learns how to use the witcher senses to locate objects, how to climb and jump, the basics of swordplay such as how to perform quick attacks, parry incoming blows, and use a variety of Witcher signs to gain an edge in combat. Experienced players can skip the tutorial and begin the game immediately but the tutorial part serves an important purpose for the inexperienced: it reduces complexity and increases playability.

Playability can also be defined as sending player actions to the virtual world using input units and then getting the desired output. Quality of the story, reactivity and usability of the system, personalization choices, control, the intensity of inter-action, the realism level, and the quality of graphics and voice are factors that affect playability (Sánchez et al. 2012). Another study defined the three criteria that affect playability as: the mechanics (rules, goals, and aims), the story (storytelling tech-nique and main theme), and interaction (elements that the player can interact with) (Rollings and Adams 2003). In this regard, *The Witcher 3: Wild Hunt* provides a high quality story, a reactive and usable environment, realistic graphics and voices, and a sense of control over a highly interactive virtual world. Game designers also use different techniques to motivate the player and to set up an atmosphere. Various sound effects and soundtracks played throughout the game as well as the adjust-ments of lighting serve these purposes but it should be noted that these techniques should not restrain player interactions. If the player is unable to hear the sounds because of a song played too loud or if he/she is unable to see his/her surroundings because of poor lighting, the virtual world may lose its believability and the play-ability will also decline. But these techniques, if they are finely tuned without affecting playability, will increase the believability of the virtual world and will also help the user to concentrate on the game.

According to Crawford (1982) attempts to increase graphical realism usually affects playability. A computer game with realistic graphics will require the latest hardware to run on and it is playable for those that own the hardware components. *The Witcher 3: Wild Hunt*'s minimum requirements are: an Intel Core i5-2500 k CPU, 6 GB of ram, NVIDIA GPU GeForce GTX 660 or AMD GPU Radeon HD 7870 graphics card, and 40 GB of free disk space. For any player that does not meet these requirements, the game is not playable. If the graphical realism starts to affect the player satisfaction and the playability of the game, designers should consider reducing graphical realism. A game that looks perfect on the screen is as good as it is playable. *The Witcher 3: Wild Hunt* provides breathtaking views from the very beginning of the game but the game suffers long loading times and sometimes crashes during gameplay. The graphics may be perfect but even the latest consoles are having difficulties to load it immediately, which breaks the immersion of the player and affects playability.

Players should also be given context-sensitive help while playing so that they do not get stuck or have to rely on a manual (Desurvire et al. 2004). This will also increase believability and reduce uncertainty for the player. Players can set an active quest in *The Witcher 3: Wild Hunt* to guide themselves toward their goal in a mas-sive world map. They can also lock on a target in the map so that they will be able to find it easily. Witcher senses are also very useful in inspecting crime scenes and following trails. The quests log also shows the level requirement for finishing them, giving the player an idea about how easy or how difficult a quest will be. Enemies those are too difficult for the player have a red skull floating above them, hinting of danger before the player engages them. Locations of interest are highlighted with various symbols on the map so that the player will have an idea where the nearest blacksmith, inn, monster nest, or place of power is (Fig. 7.4).

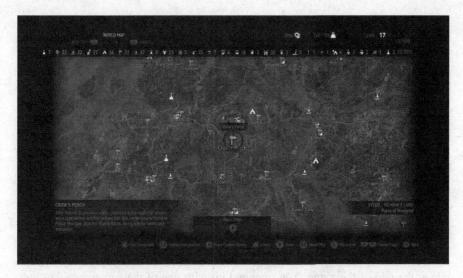

Fig. 7.4 World map of Velen—No Man's Land (with permission of CD Projekt Red)

7.4   Satisfaction/Fun

> You can have the greatest design document ever made, and you're going to change 90
> percent of it as soon as you play the game. Great games are played not made.[4]
>
> Todd Howard, Game Designer (Fallout and Elder Scrolls series)

User satisfaction in virtual environments depends on the aim of the design. Educational virtual environments will have a different notion than those designed for entertainment purposes. Since digital games are based on winning or losing, designers have to decide how hard or easy it is to win. The delicate balance between difficulty and satisfaction is closely related with gamer characteristics. Experienced players will find easily solved problems boring and inexperienced players will lose their motivation to play if the game is too difficult for them. If the designers aim to satisfy the whole gamer population, they have to balance the difficulty of the game accordingly and the core of satisfaction is a task that can be finished. The player should be able to concentrate on this task and clear goals, as well as immediate feedback, should facilitate user concentration. Focus and concentration also strips the player of his/her daily stress by altering the notion of time. And if the player believes that he/she has control over the virtual world, the state of flow and therefore increased satisfaction arise (Csikszentmihalyi 1990).

Concentration, one of the primary components of satisfaction, is the degree of player focus on the virtual. For a higher concentration, the game should stimulate the player from different sources, the stimuli should be remarkable, the virtual world should not distract but attract attention, the missions or quests should be

---

[4] http://www.gamasutra.com/view/news/113368/DICE_09_Bethesdas_Howard_On_Supreme_ Playability.php

worthy of doing, and the system should constantly provide feedback but consider the sensual, cognitive, and memory constraints of the player (Sweetser and Wyeth 2005). Sense of control over the virtual world and its inhabitants is also crucial. Players should feel that their actions and choices are changing or affecting the world. Additionally, the player should have the opportunity to stop, save, and load the game. Since irrevocable mistakes may diminish user satisfaction, the players should be given opportunities for redemption. Losing is of course a natural part of any computer game but the player should be able to adjust how frequently he/she loses by selecting a difficulty for the game. *The Witcher 3: Wild Hunt* provides many choices for the player throughout the game and it is very difficult to predict the possible consequences for these choices. Maybe it is this uncertainty, the resemblance of the game choices to their real-life counterparts that makes the game so popular. For example, the game provides two major romance choices for the player: Triss Merigold and Yennefer of Vengerberg. During various quests, the player spends time with both sorceresses and has to be careful with the dialogue choices because the overall story will have a romance arc defining what will happen at the end of the game. You may end up with one of the sorceresses but you may also lose both if you are dishonest and unfaithful to them.

Since player dissatisfaction is to be avoided at all costs, the designers use different techniques to satisfy different types of players. Difficulty may be chosen by the player but it may also be finely tuned automatically the system. Artificial intelligence will observe the player throughout the game and will try to avoid situations where the game is too difficult or too easy for the player (Hunicke and Chapman 2004). These dynamic difficulty adjustments coupled with dynamic rewarding systems may satisfy some players and it may also annoy some others. Therefore, the choice of adjusting the difficulty or rewards dynamically should also be left to the players; they should be able to turn it on or off. For example, the world of *The Witcher 3: Wild Hunt* has many bandit camps and the bandits encountered at the beginning of the game are much easier than those encountered at regions opened toward the end of the game. This brings the obvious question in mind: why are the bandits of Skellige Isles more powerful than the ones in Velen? Is there a policy or agreement among bandits that enforces the powerful to go to Skellige Isles and the latter to stay in Velen? The dynamic adjustment of opponent stats and equipment, when it is too obvious, may break the sense of immersion and dissatisfy some players (Fig. 7.5).

It is also very important to know what kinds of different players are out there if you are planning to satisfy them all. The most prominent and popular study in this regard belongs to Richard Bartle (2004) which defines four different types of players. Killers like to provoke and cause drama and/or impose them over other players in the scope provided by the virtual world. Achievers are competitive and enjoy beating difficult challenges whether they are set by the game or by themselves. Explorers like to explore the world—not just its geography but also the finer details of the game mechanics. Socializers are often more interested in having relations with the other players than playing the game itself. These player types have never been empirically tested to validate that they are independent of each other and a player may behave like more than one type during a computer game. But studies on player types provide a guideline for designers, pointing out to different player moti-

Fig. 7.5 Geralt fighting with bandits (with permission of CD Projekt Red)

vations or playstyles that can be satisfied with different gaming situations. Nevertheless, a player model that takes into account motivations, underlying processes, personality traits, general behavior patterns, and corresponding individual actions may yield better results in grouping player preferences (Bostan 2009).

7.5   Presence/Immersion

What I'm going for is the creation of a realistic virtual world, where you can feel heat, moisture, the air, and to do that what we do is have rain, we have steam, we have breath, we have blurs, so we use our graphic skills there, to make the player feel all these things.[5]

Hideo Kojima, Video Game Designer

Presence, which is defined as the subjective experience of being there, is a psychological phenomenon that resides in the perceptions of the user. As well as being defined as the perceptual illusion of being in a virtual environment by means of a communication medium, presence is highly dependent on how users interpret and experience the virtual world. Research on the psychological dimensions of presence (Ijsselsteijn 2002; Regenbrecht et al. 1998; Waterworth 2003; Ijsselsteijn and Riva 2003; Riva 2004) has defined it as a biological phenomenon, a neuropsychological process, and a product of consciousness that relies on perceptual-motor abilities, mental states, traits, needs, preferences, and experience of the user. It is a feeling and an activity of selective attention that originates from filtering and organizing conflicting sensory data taken from the real and virtual worlds. It depends on how the user perceives the world, how the user allocates his/her attention, and how he/

[5] http://www.ign.com/articles/2000/05/16/e3-hideo-kojima-interview

she maintains a mental structure of the world. And like all human experiences, it is also influenced by emotions. Interaction with other characters and interpretation of a story/scene in the virtual world will invoke different emotions in different users, and is dependent on various user characteristics such as age, gender, personality traits, background, and so on.

An important term closely related with presence is immersion. Immersion is defined by Slater and Wilbur (1997) as a system's ability to deliver a surrounding virtual environment, capable of shutting down the sensations from the real world. According to Ermi and Mäyrä (2005), immersion in computer games has three dimensions. Sensory immersion is related to audiovisual properties of the virtual world, challenge-based immersion is related with mental skills such as strategic thinking or logical problem solving, and imaginative immersion is related with the storyline and virtual characters. Playing a computer game with a desktop computer and a monitor can be described as looking into the virtual from a window of the real world. The player experiences the stimuli of both the real and the virtual which damages the sense of immersion. Virtual reality headsets or head-mounted displays are devices capable of shutting the sensations from the real world, allowing the user to concentrate on the virtual. These devices once belong to the research laboratories but they are also gaining attention as entertainment products now. The Oculus Rift virtual reality headset has been the talk of the tech world for a very long time and Oculus has described it as "the first really professional PC-based VR headset." Sony Corp. also announced its own vision of virtual reality headset—Morpheus—at GDC 2014: the 2014 (annual) Game Developers Conference. The future of gaming relies on a stronger sense of presence and immersion.

The realism of the virtual world is closely related with the sense of presence. As the player believes more in belonging to a virtual world, the line between the real and the virtual also blur. This brings up a few questions in mind: what are the factors that contribute to a sense of presence? How personal differences between players affect it? Is immersion enough for a sense of presence or are there other significant factors? Is it possible to experience a sense of presence without a virtual reality headset through focusing attention on the virtual and concentrating on the task? These questions still need answers but the critical component of the sense of presence in computer games is interaction. Presence can also be experienced while reading a book or watching a movie but playing a game is not a passive activity and this distinctive feature is the key to user satisfaction (Fig. 7.6).

One of the most important studies on the dimensions of presence was conducted by Heeter (1992), who classified the concept into three components: personal presence, social presence, and environmental presence. Virtual reality systems mainly focus on personal presence, with the aim of creating artificial sensory information similar to the stimuli human senses detect and interpret in the real world. Personal or physical presence represents the sense of being physically inside a virtual world where the design of the protagonist comes into prominence. The physical modeling, the voice acting, and the personality of this character determine the level of personal or physical presence for the player. And in this regard, *The Witcher 3: Wild Hunt* perfectly exemplifies how a believable protagonist should be designed. Although Geralt of Rivia is definitely a tough guy with a bit of the stoic, rugged hero about him, he perfectly blends into the

Fig. 7.6 Sunset at the Fields of Ard Skellig (with permission of CD Projekt Red)

gloomy and desperate world he is wandering in. The second component, social presence, represents the user's ability to communicate interactively with users or computer-
generated agents within the virtual world; and environmental presence represents the
user's ability to change the virtual world by his or her actions. If objects within the
virtual world do not react to the user's actions, then the virtual environment does not
constitute a realistic simulation. In this sense, computer games are artificial universes
that rely on personal, social, and environmental presence.

7.6   Freedom/Choice

> The presence of a choice that I know is there that I didn't take is still valuable by virtue of
> the fact that I could have taken it, someone else took it instead and that's how I know that I
> had freedom of choice and that my choices had meaning. That's a value of its own.[6]
>
>   Tim Stellmach, Lead Designer of OtherSide Entertainment

Freedom of choice can be described as providing the player a range of choices so
that he/she may select one. Not only the number of choices but how much the
choices satisfy the player is important. Choices are usually associated with stories
but it can also be argued that every key press or every mouse click is a choice. In the
context of stories, some games provide linear storylines where the player has almost
no effect to the progression of events. Others have branching storylines where
player choices do have an impact and the story takes different turns according to
player choices. Open world systems, which provide massive worlds with hundreds
of locations, characters, and quests, provide the illusionary sense of freedom

---

[6] http://www.rpgcodex.net/content.php?id=9788

successfully. But it should be noted that too much freedom may mislead the player from the main story and the player may find himself wandering aimlessly in a world of too many things that get his/her attention.

The player may not have any impact on the story or the virtual world if everything is strictly determined by the designers. The order of cities or the regions that the player will visit cannot be changed and the player is merely a spectator wandering inside an interactive world which is not so interactive. Since the story is not responding to player actions or choices, interaction seems like losing its meaning. But it should be noted that games are not stories and the storyline is not the only element that reinforces player satisfaction. Many computer games provide linear storylines but they provide believable environments with believable characters that entertain the player. *The Witcher 3: Wild Hunt* provides a massive world with hundreds of different locations to visit, providing a new quest or a new character in every location but it is not only this freedom that makes the game so interesting. The cities, the society, the characters, the conflicts, and the quests are perfectly blended together into a believable world (Fig. 7.7).

When a computer game provides good/evil or black/white choices, it is much easier to make a choice. The distinctions are very clear and the player can predict which dialogue option or action will lead to his goal. But *The Witcher* series always provided vague choices where the line between good and evil began to blur. There are always serious moral choices and the characters are not good or bad stereotypes but they are alike the real people that we encounter in our lives. The protagonist of the game, Geralt of Rivia, is often criticized or blamed in his choices. The player is responsible as the moral compass of Geralt and can choose what kind of a man he will be. For example, Trollololo is a rock troll recruited into the Redanian Army who was ordered to guard the boats taken from peasants. But when the peasants came to get their boats back, the guards arrived to stop them from doing so. Then when the troll tried to calmly separate them, he accidentally killed them all. When left with the bodies, he figured the best solution was to cook them all in a stew. So, what will the player do to this rock troll who is still guarding the remaining boats dutifully? Does he deserve death simply because he is a monster? Is he worse or better than the human soldiers of war who plunder, kill, and rape? And he enthusiastically sings a Redanian marching tune!

The integration of the virtual world and the player is also a requirement for a sense of freedom. First of all, the player should feel himself part of the virtual world and he/she should know why he/she is there. Otherwise the player will question his/her existence and his/her choices will lose their meaning. Game players usually find themselves in hostile environments where enemies or monsters attacked them but there should be an explanation about where the player is, what kind of a world he/she stepped into, who is enemy and who is friend, and why? If these questions are not answered, regardless of the choices and the freedom the game offers, the virtual world will lose its believability and therefore its meaning. Opening cinematic of video games usually answer some of these questions so that the player will be motivated to play the role of the protagonist. In this regard, the

Fig. 7.7 Friendly chat with Trollololo (with permission of CD Projekt Red)

Fig. 7.8 Screenshot from the opening cinematic (with permission of CD Projekt Red)

opening cinematic of the *Witcher 3: Wild Hunt*, where a priest of the Church of Eternal Fire preaches the common folk, is very successful (Fig. 7.8).

> ...In a time past our world intertwined with another through an upheaval scholars call the Conjunction of the Spheres. The Gods allowed unholy forces to slip into our domain. The offspring of that cataclysm was the nefarious force called 'Magic'. Yet we did not banish it. Instead studying the vile arkane for our own power and wealth. And the monsters at our

door, the unholy relics of this Conjunction - the trolls, the corpse eaters, the werewolves - did we raise our swords against them? Or have we laid this burden on others? On so called – 'Witchers'. Stray children taught the ways of foul sorcery. Their bodies mutated through blasphemous ritual. Sent to fight monsters though they could not distinguish good from evil. The flicker of humanity long extinguished within them. Yes, their numbers have dwindled through the years. But a few still roam our lands offering their bloody work for coin. To this day they shame us with their very existence. The North bleeds, flogged by war. The battles are the Gods' whip, chastisement for our sins. And let us not forget the terrors that scourges from beyond our world. The Wild Hunt rides the sky with every full moon. The dark reign has abduct our children into lands unknown…

The launch cinematic—"A Night to Remember"—which perfectly describes what a monster contract is and how a witcher uses his powers, weapons, and potions to defeat a monster, has received the prestigious 2015 animago AWARD for "Best Trailer/Opener".[7] Even the trailer of the game sets up the atmosphere for the players before the game was released.

7.7 Conclusion

Computer game design is not only about algorithms, scripts, and logic. Games are interactive environments and gamers are humans, so it should be remembered that gamer interaction is a social phenomenon and the psychological components that underlie the concept of stepping into an alternative reality cannot be ignored. The realism, playability, believability of the virtual world, as well as player enjoyment or fun are important design requirements. The player should feel himself in the world mediated by the computer and should believe that he/she exists there. The player should also feel a sense of control over the events and should think that he/she can affect the virtual environment. Looking into a game from the player's perspective is very important if your aim is to design the games that players want, not the games that the designers want to design.

References

Bartle RA (2004) Designing virtual worlds. New Riders Publishing
Bostan B (2009) Player motivations: a psychological perspective. ACM Comput Entertain 7(2). http://dl.acm.org/citation.cfm?doid=1541895.1541902
Cheng K, Cairns P (2005) Behaviour, realism and immersion in games. ACM conference on human factors in computing systems, CHI 2005, ACM, pp 1272–1275
Crawford C (1982) The art of computer game design. Osborne/McGraw Hill, Berkeley
Csikszentmihalyi M (1990) Flow: the psychology of optimal experience. Harper Perennial, New York

---

[7] 15 October 2015, http://www.animago.com/en/news/archiv/congratulations-here-are-the-2015-animago-award-winners/

Desurvire H, Caplan M, Toth JA (2004) Using heuristics to evaluate the playability of games. CHI '04 extended abstracts on human factors in computing systems (Vienna, Austria, April 24–29, 2004). CHI '04. ACM, New York, pp 1509–1512

Ermi L, Mäyrä F (2005) Fundamental components of the gameplay experience: analysing immersion. Paper presented at DIGRA 2005: changing views: worlds in play, Vancouver, Canada

Heeter C (1992) Being there: the subjective experience of presence. Presence Teleop Virt Environ 1(2):262–271

Hunicke R, Chapman V (2004) AI for dynamic difficulty adjustment in games. Challenges in game artificial intelligence AAAI workshop, San Jose, pp 91–96

Ijsselsteijn WA (2002) Elements of a multi-level theory of presence: phenomenology, mental processing and neural correlates. In: Proceedings of presence 2002, 9–11

Ijsselsteijn W, Riva G (2003) Being there: the experience of presence in mediated environments. In: Riva G, Davide F, Ijsselsteijn WA (eds) Being there: concepts, effects and measurement of user presence in synthetic environments. IOS, Amsterdam

Kamal B (2003) Believability in computer games. IE2004 Australian workshop on interactive entertainment, Sydney

Laurel B (1993) Computers as theatre. Addison-Wesley, Reading

Mateas M (1997) An Oz-centric review of interactive drama and believable agents. Tech Report CMU-CS-97-156, Carnegie Mellon University

Regenbrecht H, Schubert T, Friedmann F (1998) Measuring the sense of presence and its relations to fear of heights in virtual environments. Int J Hum Comput Int 10(3):233–249

Riva G (2004) The psychology of ambient intelligence: activity, situation and presence. In: Riva G, Davide F, Vatalaro F, Alcañiz M (eds) Ambient Intelligence: the evolution of technology, communication and cognition towards the future of the human-computer interaction. IOS, Amsterdam

Rollings A, Adams E (2003) Andrew Rollings and Ernest Adams on game design. New Riders Games, Indianapolis

Sánchez JLG, Vela FLG, Simarro FM, Padilla-Zea N (2012) Playability: analysing user experience in video games. Behav Inf Technol 31(10):1033–1054

Slater M, Wilbur S (1997) A framework for immersive virtual environments (FIVE): speculations on the role of presence in virtual environments. Presence Teleop Virt Environ 6(6):603–616

Storms RL, Zyda MJ (2000) Interactions in perceived quality of auditory-visual displays. Presence 9(6):557–580

Sweetser P, Wyeth P (2005) GameFlow: a model for evaluating player enjoyment in games. ACM Comput Entertain 3(3). http://dl.acm.org/citation.cfm?doid=1077246.1077253

Waterworth EL (2003) The meaning of presence. Presence Connect 3(3). http://www8.informatik.umu.se/~jwworth/PRESENCE-meaning.htm

Chapter 8
Self-Determination Theory in Digital Games

Ahmet Uysal and Irem Gokce Yildirim

Abstract Self-determination theory (SDT; Intrinsic motivation and self-determination in human behavior, New York, 1985; The oxford handbook of human motivation, New York, pp 85–107, 2012) is a broad motivational theory that has been developing for the last four decades. The theory makes the distinction between intrinsic and extrinsic motivation and identifies three basic psychological needs that are essential for well-being. When people are intrinsically motivated, they engage in an activity because the activity itself is interesting, enjoyable, and congruent with their selves. In contrast, when people are extrinsically motivated, they engage in an activity because the activity is instrumental in obtaining rewards or avoiding punishments. In this chapter, we will discuss digital games within a SDT framework, with a focus on how satisfaction of basic psychological needs in games can enhance user experience. We start with the behavioral psychology principles and the use of rewards in games that fuel extrinsic motivation. Next, we discuss intrinsic–extrinsic motivation and the three basic psychological needs—autonomy, competence, and relatedness—that facilitate intrinsic motivation and enhance player experience. Finally, we discuss some basic game features and their relation to basic needs.

Keywords Digital games • Motivation • Self-determination theory

A. Uysal, Ph.D. (✉)
Department of Psychology, Middle East Technical University, Ankara, Turkey
e-mail: uahmet@metu.edu.tr

I.G. Yildirim, M.S.
Game Technologies Program, Informatics Institute, Middle East Technical University,
Ankara, Turkey
e-mail: iremgokceyildirim@gmail.com

© Springer International Publishing Switzerland 2016
B. Bostan (ed.), *Gamer Psychology and Behavior*, International Series
on Computer Entertainment and Media Technology,
DOI 10.1007/978-3-319-29904-4_8

8.1 Behavioral Psychology

Behaviorism was the dominant view in mainstream psychology until the 1960s. This school of thought was based on the idea that psychology should only study observable and measurable behavior, and rejected the idea that the mind or cognitive processes can be studied scientifically. Although mainstream psychology moved away from behaviorism, basic principles of behavioral psychology are commonly used in games, and they provide some insight about gamer behaviors. Moreover, these principles are important to understand the intrinsic and extrinsic motivation distinction.

According to the operant theory (Skinner 1953), behaviors are learned and motivated by rewards and punishments. That is, behaviors that are reinforced will be strengthened, whereas behaviors that are punished will be extinguished. For example, a pigeon that is rewarded with a food pellet each time after pecking a button when a light turns green will eventually learn to peck the button when it sees the green light. Thus, desired behaviors can be taught and motivated by rewards. Behaviorist approach also suggests that human behaviors operate similarly, and our behaviors are conditioned via various types of reinforcements (social, material, etc.) and punishments.

8.1.1 Schedules of Reinforcement and Games

In order to reinforce a behavior, rewards can be provided contingent on a number of responses or contingent on a time interval (Ferster and Skinner 1957). For example, the pigeon may receive a food pellet every fifth time it presses the button, or after variable number of button presses. Similarly, the pigeon may receive the food once in every 2 min, or once after variable number of minutes passed.

These different types of requirements for the delivery of reinforcement are labeled as schedules of reinforcement. Apart from continuous reinforcement, where a behavior is rewarded every time, there are four basic types of reinforcement schedules. Number of response-contingent ones are called ratio schedules, whereas, time-contingent ones are called interval schedules.

A fixed ratio schedule indicates that the response will be reinforced after a fixed number of responses. In our pigeon example, a pigeon on a fixed ratio 5 (FR 5) schedule would receive a food pellet each time after pecking the button five times. This kind of schedule results in a high rate of response (pecking the button), with a short pause after the reinforcement (food), which is called a "break and run pattern."

Fixed ratio schedule is used in games frequently. Some basic examples are killing a fixed number of monsters (response) to level up (reinforcement), or collecting a fixed number of items to increase the player's health bar. A fixed ratio 1 is a continuous reinforcement, and probably the most common type of schedule used in games. Gaining points, experience, or special rewards each time after certain game actions are some examples of continuous reinforcement. The break pattern after reinforcement can happen outside or within the game. For instance, in an RPG game, a player is more likely to keep playing until her character reaches the next level or finishes a quest before taking a break. These breaks can also take place within the game's world. For instance, if this is an open world game that allows exploration, the player initially may focus on obtaining the rewards provided by the quests, and then explore the game's world for some time before returning back to questing.

A variable ratio schedule indicates that the response will be reinforced after an unpredictable number of responses, within a set average response rate. For instance, a pigeon on a VR5 schedule might receive the first food pellet after 4 pecks, the second one after 10 pecks, and the third one after 1 peck, averaging to 5 responses for each reinforcer. This kind of schedule results in a high rate steady response pattern (linear) with very brief or no breaks.

A classic example of variable ratio schedule is gambling or lottery games. For example, slot machines use this kind of schedule that results in a very high response rate. As the players know they will eventually win, they keep playing to receive the reward. After receiving the reward, there is still the possibility that the next coin may also produce rewards. In digital games, "loots" are generally based on a variable ratio schedule. The players do not know how many creatures they have to kill before obtaining the special item that these creatures drop. Moreover, the players may even find the task boring, but the probability of obtaining the special reward results in a steady high response rate. Similarly, simple Facebook games also frequently use variable ratio schedules (Lewis et al. 2012).

A fixed interval schedule indicates that the response will be reinforced after a fixed period of time. For example, a pigeon on a one minute fixed interval schedule will receive food for its first peck after 1 minute elapses. Another minute needs to pass before the second food is delivered, and any number of pecks in between is not rewarded. Fixed interval schedules lead to a longer pause after the reinforcement and a gradually increasing response rate (i.e., a scalloped curve) as the reinforcement time approaches.

Browser games and Facebook games use this kind of schedule frequently. For instance, the game can provide various rewards for logging in once within a fixed time period. This could be a positive reinforcer such as a reward (e.g., daily in-game currency reward for logging in) or a negative reinforcer such as preventing an undesirable outcome (renewing the magical shield of your city, protecting your space fleet, protecting your crops from withering, etc.). The response pattern is a gradually increasing curve. For example, a game can reward the player for logging in every three hours. The player will log in to receive the reward, do something else for a couple of hours, and start checking the game more and more frequently until the next interval's reward is available (unless there is a countdown timer in the game, but then checking the timer may become more frequent).

Fixed interval schedules are especially effective for negative reinforcers in games. For instance, on Clash of Clans wiki website, a player inquires "Can I keep myself from being attacked by always staying online and active; presuming that I got something to touch my device once per minute?" Another player responds "Yes you can, in fact I've seen many people do this." Some free-to-play games take advantage of this schedule. These games are free, but the player is not allowed to do highly rewarding game actions until a fixed amount of time passes, unless the player pays real money. The players can receive the reward immediately, instead of waiting for the fixed interval, if they pay. The case of the Facebook application "Cow Clicker" is an ironic example for the potency of fixed interval schedules, which is discussed thoroughly by Lewis et al. (2012).

A variable interval schedule indicates that the response will be reinforced after an unpredictable period of time, within a previously set average period. For instance, on a 15 minute variable interval schedule, the response is reinforced in variable time periods that would average up to 15 minutes. Variable interval schedules result in a moderate steady response rate with very brief or no pauses. The response rate of variable interval schedule is less steep than that of variable ratio schedule. In fact, interval schedules in general result in lower response rates than ratio schedules.

In games, variable interval schedules can also be used instead of fixed interval or variable ratio schedules. For instance, in an MMO game, a special quest might become available based on a variable interval schedule. Similarly, browser game examples discussed above can also use variable interval schedules.

8.2   Self-Determination Theory and the Undermining Effect of Rewards on Intrinsic Motivation

According to the self-determination theory (SDT) (Deci and Ryan 1985), extrinsic motivation is defined as doing an activity to obtain an outcome that is separable from the activity. Thus, operant theory principles we discussed above fall under extrinsic motivation. Intrinsic motivation, in contrast, entails engaging in an activity because it is inherently interesting and satisfactory. These activities are volitional, lead to feelings of being effective, and provide opportunities for growth (Ryan and Deci 2000a). SDT also states that people have an inherent tendency toward intrinsically motivated activities and growth.

Research on SDT began with the controversial finding that rewards could have a negative effect on intrinsic motivation (Deci 1971). Initial study with university students showed that monetary rewards decreased intrinsic motivation for an interesting activity. The findings were subsequently replicated with preschoolers using symbolic rewards (Lepper et al. 1973). Research on this topic continued in the following years showing that in addition to tangible rewards, threats (Deci and Cascio 1972), deadlines (Amabile et al. 1976), and directives (Koestner et al. 1984) can also decrease intrinsic motivation. This negative effect of reinforcers on intrinsic motivation was labeled as the undermining effect (Deci and Ryan 1980).

However, the issue remained to be controversial as Eisenberger and Cameron (1996) conducted a meta-analysis concluding that undermining effect is a myth and these detrimental effects occur under highly restrictive conditions. In response, Deci et al. (1999) conducted an extensive meta-analysis of 128 studies, concluding that the undermining effect is a reality and the meta-analysis of Eisenberger and colleagues had methodological problems along with misunderstandings of SDT.

Rewards can have a negative effect on intrinsic motivation, but not all rewards are undermining. According to SDT, rewards have an informational and a controlling aspect, and their effect on intrinsic motivation depends on which aspect is perceived as more salient. Informational aspect of rewards refers to their role as performance or competence feedback. When this aspect is salient, rewards maintain or enhance intrinsic motivation. In contrast, the controlling aspect of rewards refers to their role as an instrument for controlling people's behavior. When this aspect is salient, rewards undermine intrinsic motivation (Ryan and Deci 2000a). In general, expected tangible rewards such as money or awards tend to undermine intrinsic motivation. In contrast, verbal rewards such as positive feedback or praise tend to enhance intrinsic motivation (Deci et al. 1999).

8.2.1   Intrinsic and Extrinsic Motivation in Games

At a first glance, intrinsic motivation seems like the essential element of games. Why would people play a game if they do not find it interesting and they are not having fun? However, as we discussed in the first section of this article, games can put people in a Skinner box. People do play games with extrinsic motivation for reasons such as gaining in-game awards and prestige (Lafrenière et al. 2012). Moreover, there could be extrinsically motivated sections within a game, even if the overall motivation for playing the game is not extrinsic. In fact, player terms such as "grinding" or "farming" refer to these activities that are merely done to obtain the rewards. Thus, whether such extrinsic rewards also undermine intrinsic motivation in games is an important question. In the recent years, researchers began to investigate intrinsic and extrinsic motivation in games; however, the literature on this topic is still limited.

In an experimental study, researchers investigated the effect of feedback valence and type of feedback (descriptive, evaluative, comparative) on intrinsic motivation (Burgers et al. 2015). It was found that positive feedback increased intrinsic motivation as the players felt more competent and autonomous (these constructs are discussed in the following section). Negative feedback, however, increased the desire to play the game immediately, probably as an effort to repair low performance. Feedback type did not have a significant effect on intrinsic motivation and the findings regarding future play were mixed.

Modern games also make use of meta-rewards such as achievements, badges, or trophies. These are rewards that are generally given for completing a game objective. Furthermore, the platforms using these rewards (e.g., PlayStation, Xbox, and Steam) allow displaying or comparison of these rewards to other players. A recent qualitative study examined the motivational aspects of meta-rewards (Cruz et al. in press). After conducting focus groups, researchers concluded that achievement badges can be perceived as informational or controlling rewards, lead to gameplay experimentation, create feelings of competence, maintain or boost ego, and act as social status or skill indicators. Some players also reported feeling compelled to earn all available rewards. It seems there are some intrinsic aspects of meta-reward systems such as their competence supporting and gameplay experimentation properties, as well as, extrinsic aspects such as ego-maintenance or social comparison properties. The extrinsic aspects of meta-reward systems are likely to extend play time, but also likely to undermine intrinsic motivation and game enjoyment.

Similarly, gamification in nondigital contexts also uses meta-rewards. Although the findings regarding effectiveness of gamification are mixed and dependent on various factors (Hamari et al. 2014), a more recent longitudinal study addressing some of the shortcomings of previous studies on gamification found that use of badges in educational settings (along with other gamification elements) lowered intrinsic motivation, course satisfaction, and course grades compared to the non-gamified control classroom (Hanus and Fox 2015). In another similar study, badges did not decrease student's motivation, interest, and engagement, but increased their understanding in an educational game (Filsecker and Hickey 2014). However, researchers concluded that badges provided in the game were unexpected and emphasized their informational aspect rather than controlling aspect; therefore, they did not undermine intrinsic motivation.

From a game designer's perspective, it might be suggested that it does not matter whether a player is extrinsically or intrinsically motivated, as long as the players are motivated. However, designers need to be aware of the consequences of extrinsically motivated game playing. For example, research shows that extrinsic reasons for playing a game such as playing apathetically, obtaining in-game rewards and items, gaining social recognition, and release of tension or guilt significantly predict excessive and problem gaming (King and Delfabbro 2009). Similarly, extrinsic motivation for playing games is linked with obsessive passion, an unhealthy type of passion in which the person feels compelled to engage in the activity that contradicts with other aspects of one's life, as opposed to harmonious passion that is more self-determined and generally leads to positive outcomes (Przybylski et al. 2009a, b; Wang et al. 2008). Thus, these findings suggest that extrinsic motivation in games can increase playing time with a cost to well-being of players.

In sum, the undermining effect of extrinsic rewards in games depends on whether they are perceived as controlling or informational. Furthermore, there is no doubt that use of operant theory principles increases extrinsic motivation, play time, and could even lead to addictive playing. Player communities invented words such as grinding and farming that refer to doing the same in-game action over and over again to obtain the desired reward that is on a type of schedule of reinforcement. However, these words also have negative connotations. Anecdotal evidence suggests that players find these sections dull and boring, something they "have to" do to obtain the reward. How these sections of games have an effect on player's intrinsic motivation and overall game experience is yet to be investigated empirically. Nevertheless, intrinsic motivation is essential for enjoyment and fun. We now turn our attention to how intrinsic motivation can be facilitated in games.

8.2.2 Basic Psychological Needs

According to SDT, people have three basic psychological needs—autonomy, competence, and relatedness—that are essential for well-being and psychological growth. Autonomy refers to feeling volitional in one's actions and fully endorsing them. Activities that are imposed, controlling, or in conflict with one's true self are detrimental to autonomy needs. Competence refers to feeling effective, capable, and optimally challenged. Activities that are too easy or too difficult thwart competence. In contrast, well-structured environments, skill-challenge balance, and positive performance feedback that is informational promote satisfaction of competence needs. Finally, relatedness refers to having a sense of belongingness and meaningful connection to others. Warm, supportive, and responsive environments rather than cold and neglecting ones facilitate satisfaction of relatedness needs (Ryan and Deci 2000b). According to SDT, all three needs are essential for psychological well-being and growth. Moreover, satisfaction of these needs, especially autonomy and competence needs, play a key role in intrinsic motivation. Basic needs theory has been applied to various domains including education, work, health, close relationships, sports, virtual environments, and digital games. The findings provide strong support for the propositions of the theory (for a review, see Deci and Ryan 2012).

8.2.2.1 Basic Psychological Needs in Games

Modern games with their open worlds, procedural designs, and online multiplayer features provide several opportunities to satisfy basic needs. Autonomy in digital games involves interesting options and volitional engagement (Rigby and Ryan 2011). Although having options is important for autonomy; it is still possible to feel autonomous with limited options. For example, sometimes people do not have any alternatives, but if the only available option is in accord with themselves and if they willingly engage in the activity, they still feel autonomous. Similarly, games with limited choices can still satisfy autonomy needs if it leads the player to volitionally engage in the linear path. Games that satisfy competence needs provide optimal challenges and performance feedback that lead to a sense of efficacy and mastery (Rigby and Ryan 2011). Research suggests that competence might be the most important contributor to enjoyment of games (e.g., Ryan et al. 2006; Przybylski et al. 2009a, b; Tamborini et al. 2010). Relatedness in games is generally considered in the context of multiplayer games, however, single player games with digital worlds and non-player characters (NPCs) can also facilitate satisfaction of relatedness needs. Games that make the player feel acknowledged and supported by NPCs in the virtual world satisfy relatedness needs (Rigby and Ryan 2011). Next we review the empirical research on need satisfaction in games.

In a pioneering research on this topic, four studies showed that games that satisfy autonomy, competence, and relatedness needs promote intrinsic motivation and well-being (Ryan et al. 2006). In the first study, participants completed the Player Experience of Need Satisfaction (PENS) scale which measures autonomy, competence, relatedness, intuitive game controls, and presence in game play, before and after a 20-min long Super Mario 64 play session. It was found that autonomy and competence were positively associated with enjoyment, immersion, preference for future play, and positive changes in short-term well-being. In the second study, researchers compared user experience of two commercially available games, one of which was a very popular and a high ranking game (Zelda: Ocarina of Time) and the other one had very low rankings (A Bugs Life). After two game sessions, participants found Zelda more enjoyable, immersive, and preferable for future play. More important, participants rated Zelda significantly higher in autonomy and competence scores, which predicted the differences in user experience outcomes. Third study replicated the findings using a multilevel model, thus also accounting for individual differences in players. In the last study, these associations were tested in a survey with massive multiplayer online games (MMOs) players. MMOs provide interactions between the players which can facilitate relatedness needs. Indeed, relatedness—in addition to autonomy and competence—was associated positively with presence, enjoyment, and preference for future play. Similarly, in a series of six studies that included four experiments, Przybylski et al. (2009b) investigated the associations between violent game content, need satisfaction, and player experience outcomes. All of the studies showed that autonomy and competence satisfaction in games were robustly associated with positive player experience outcomes (i.e., enjoyment, value, desire for future play), and violent content explained little or no unique variance after controlling for need satisfaction.

These findings provided strong evidence for the role of basic needs in games; however, it is not possible to draw conclusions about causal effects as none of them manipulated basic needs. Other researchers also manipulated autonomy and competence-supportive features of an exergame in a 2×2 factorial design to examine their effects on user experience outcomes (Peng et al. 2012). In the autonomy supportive condition, players could customize the appearance of their characters and choose how to develop their character's skills, and they had dialogue choices for NPC conversations. In the no-autonomy condition, none of these choices were available. In the competence-supportive condition, the game had dynamic difficulty adjustment, a heroism meter, and achievement badges for performance feedback. In the no-competence condition, none of these features were available. After a 15-minute play session, players reported their enjoyment, intrinsic motivation, self-efficacy for exercising, and their ratings for the game. Results showed that both autonomy supportive and competence supportive features resulted in a better user experience. Furthermore, need satisfaction mediated the effect of autonomy and competence-supportive game features on player experience outcomes.

These studies suggest that satisfaction of three basic needs is an important element of positive player experience and intrinsic motivation. Games that satisfy autonomy, competence, and relatedness need result in positive player experience outcomes, such as higher levels of enjoyment, immersion, intrinsic motivation, and desire for future play. In the next section, we discuss a few basic game features and their relation to satisfaction of basic needs.

8.2.2.2   Game Features and Basic Psychological Needs

Choice is an essential element of games. In fact, choices are the main interactive elements that differentiate games from other entertainment media. However, games vary in their provision of choices. Some consist of only one screen and involve limited number of choices, whereas others offer huge open worlds with lots of choices. Open world action games or role-playing games, are generally higher in autonomy satisfaction as they provide a lot of freedom to the player in developing their in-game characters, engaging in different activities or quests whenever they want. Research also suggests that providing basic choices such as avatar customization and dialogue choices increases autonomy satisfaction (Peng et al. 2012). Nevertheless, having choices is an important but not a necessary element of autonomy in games. Even if a game provides several choices, the players may still feel controlled if the game forces them to do something they do not want. In contrast, the players may still feel autonomous if the only provided choice is something they endorse. For instance, a linear game with limited number of choices can still satisfy autonomy needs if the game's narrative can create the feeling of volitional engagement in the game's linear path. Rigby and Ryan (2011) give Bioshock as an example. The game constantly tells the player what to do and provides limited choices. However, the heroic narrative makes the player willingly engage in the provided path, and this creates a sense of autonomy. In contrast, meaningless choices or choices that conflict with the game's narrative are not likely to satisfy autonomy needs. For example, Star Wars: Knights of the Old Republic II, provides the players with dark side (evil) and light side (good) choices in dialogues and quests. In one mini quest, an NPC character asks for ticket money; the light side choice is to help; and the dark side choice is to trick the character by taking all the money she has and then not buying her a ticket. The dark side choice—although evil—is incongruent with the dark side player's character, because it turns a highly feared anti-hero into a street con man. The provided options, regardless of their variety, need to be meaningful and in concordance with a player's character or the game's narrative to support autonomy.

Moreover, choices can also have an effect on competence needs. For example, providing an overwhelming number of choices can lead to a chaotic environment, as opposed to a structured one (Katz and Assor 2007). The players may feel intimidated and ineffective because of not knowing what to do. Multiplayer online battle arena games such as DOTA 2 or League of Legends could provide a good example for the negative effect of overwhelming number of choices on competence. In these team-based multiplayer battle games, new playable characters are being introduced regularly. Currently, there are more than a hundred characters, each with different in-game roles and skill trees, in addition to hundreds of items these characters can equip. Moreover, these games tend to develop a meta-game as the player community figures out the best characters for each role and their skill-item compositions. This intimidates new players, and those who try these games for the first time are likely to feel incompetent. They are put in a chaotic environment, and they do not know what to do or whether they are being effective with their choices. In contrast, for more experienced players, the choices may still feel limited because there are only a few "right" choices. In order to support autonomy and competence, choices provided to the players should be equally viable so that the players can fully endorse their choices without wondering if they are capable of choosing a good one. In fact, research suggests that choice enhances intrinsic motivation if people initially feel competent about the task, and decreases intrinsic motivation if initial perceptions of task competence are low (Patall et al. 2014).

Feedback is another basic element of games. Without feedback, the player will not be able to understand the rules and the structure of game world, how she is performing, or whether the actions have consequences or not. All of these would lead to a low sense of efficacy. Therefore, feedback in games seems to be primarily associated with competence needs. It is also associated with autonomy to some extent, because the action choices may become meaningless without feedback. Indeed, positive verbal feedback in games increases autonomy and competence satisfaction (Burgers et al. 2015). Feedback also provides information about what the player is doing right or wrong, which is essential for developing mastery and competence. For instance, in some First Person Shooter games, there is a change in the shape of the crossbar when the player aims the target correctly. This is likely to increase competence satisfaction as it provides important feedback. Games can also provide positive verbal feedback (e.g., Excellent, Killing Spree, Great) either visually or with an in-game voice for doing certain game actions. However, not all games are well designed and some of them provide vague feedback that can be detrimental to basic needs. For example, pulling a lever in a game only makes a sound (or in the worst case it just moves). The player is left wondering about what happened, whether she is doing something wrong, whether the action has a meaning or not. Sometimes this kind of feedback is used on purpose as a puzzle element. Nevertheless, in most cases vague feedback will have a negative effect on competence and autonomy needs.

A third common element is game difficulty. Difficulty creates the challenge that is essential for satisfaction of competence needs. However, games should provide an optimal level of challenge to satisfy competence needs. Too easy or too difficult games that do not match the skill level of players will lead either to boredom or frustration. Overwhelmingly difficult games are likely to result in feelings of helplessness and a giving up response, an amotivational state in SDT terms. Too easy games, in contrast, will feel boring and lose the interest of the players. Research also suggests that difficulty balancing is associated with higher levels of competence, which then predicts higher levels of enjoyment (Schmierbach et al. 2014). Similarly, in an experimental study using a multiplayer game with dynamic difficulty adjustment feature, players who were assisted by the game reported higher satisfaction of all three needs if they were unaware of the adjustment. Awareness of the adjustment still increased competence, but reduced autonomy and relatedness (Baldwin et al. 2014). Most modern games aim to provide an optimum level of challenge using features such as manually adjustable difficulty levels, introducing game actions slowly in order not to overwhelm the player, and dynamically adjusting difficulty. Even if a game is difficult, it can still satisfy competence needs if it creates a feeling of self-efficacy (I can do it the next time). However, finding the optimum difficulty could be both tricky and risky for game developers. For instance, Demon's Souls or Dark Souls series are successful games that are also notorious for their difficulty. In these action RPG games, players can die very easily, but the games also give the feeling that it is possible to overcome their challenges. This creates a tremendous sense of competence for persisting players, but many players also give up feeling frustrated.

Although not an in-game element, game controllers are also a big part of the player experience. Traditional controllers (mouse/keyboard or a game controller) will be around in the foreseeable future, but the companies are also experimenting with movement based, or more naturally mapping control methods such as Wii Remote, Microsoft's Kinect, or PlayStation's Move. With the advent of virtual reality technology, it is likely that companies will continue developing alternative controllers. A couple of studies also examined the effect of game controllers (traditional controllers vs. naturally mapped controllers) on basic needs. For example, using a realistic natural mapping controller such as racing wheel lead to highest level of autonomy compared to other controllers (McEwan et al. 2012). However, participants reported highest level of competence when using the traditional Xbox controllers. Similarly, in an experimental study, participants either played a bowling game with a natural mapping controller (Nintendo WiiMote encased in a plastic bowling bowl) or a traditional PlayStation controller. Results showed that natural mapping controller resulted in higher levels of autonomy and competence satisfaction, which in turn predicted game enjoyment (Tamborini et al. 2010).

8.3 Conclusion

In conclusion, SDT provides a concise framework to understand the motivational aspects of gamer psychology. Moreover, it also identifies three basic needs that facilitate fun in games. Game designers should focus on implementing game mechanics that support autonomy, competence, and relatedness needs to enhance the player experience.

References

Amabile TM, DeJong W, Lepper MR (1976) Effects of externally imposed deadlines on subsequent intrinsic motivation. J Pers Soc Psychol 34(1):92–98

Baldwin A, Johnson D, Wyeth PA (2014) The effect of multiplayer dynamic difficulty adjustment on the player experience of video games. In: Proceedings of the CHI '14 extended abstracts on human factors in computing systems. ACM, New York, pp 1489–1494

Burgers C, Eden A, van Engelenburg MD, Buningh S (2015) How feedback boosts motivation and play in a brain-training game. Comput Hum Behav 48:94–103

Cruz C, Hanus MD, Fox J (2015) The need to achieve: players' perceptions and uses of extrinsic meta-game reward systems for video game consoles. Comput Hum Behav. doi:10.1016/j.chb.2015.08.017

Deci EL (1971) Effects of externally mediated rewards on intrinsic motivation. J Pers Soc Psychol 18(1):105–115

Deci EL, Cascio WF (1972) Changes in intrinsic motivation as a function of negative feedback and threats. Paper presented at the Eastern Psychological Association, Boston, MA

Deci EL, Ryan RM (1980) The empirical exploration of intrinsic motivational processes. In: Berkowitz L (ed) Advances in experimental social psychology. Academic Press, New York, pp 39–80

Deci EL, Ryan RM (1985) Intrinsic motivation and self-determination in human behavior. Plenum, New York

Deci EL, Ryan RM (2012) Motivation, personality, and development within embedded social contexts: an overview of self-determination theory. In: Ryan RM (ed) The oxford handbook of human motivation. Oxford University Press, New York, pp 85–107

Deci EL, Koestner R, Ryan RM (1999) A meta-analytic review of experiments examining the effects of extrinsic rewards on intrinsic motivation. Psychol Bull 125(6):627–668

Eisenberger R, Cameron J (1996) Detrimental effects of reward: reality or myth? Am Psychol 51(11):1153–1166

Ferster CB, Skinner BF (1957) Schedules of reinforcement. Appleton-Century-Crofts, New York

Filsecker M, Hickey DT (2014) A multilevel analysis of the effects of external rewards on elementary students' motivation, engagement and learning in an educational game. Comput Educ 75:136–148

Hamari J, Koivisto J, Sarsa H (2014) Does gamification work?—a literature review of empirical studies on gamification. In Proceedings of the 47th Hawaii international conference on system sciences, IEEE, Hawaii, pp 3025–3034

Hanus MD, Fox J (2015) Assessing the effects of gamification in the classroom: a longitudinal study on intrinsic motivation, social comparison, satisfaction, effort, and academic performance. Comput Educ 80:152–161

Katz I, Assor A (2007) When choice motivates and when it does not. Educ Psychol Rev 19:429–442

King D, Delfabbro P (2009) Motivational differences in problem video game play. J Cyber Ther Rehab 2(2):139–149

Koestner R, Ryan RM, Bernieri F, Holt K (1984) Setting limits on children's behavior: the differential effects of controlling vs. informational styles on intrinsic motivation and creativity. J Pers 52(3):233–248

Lafrenière MK, Verner-Filion J, Vallerand RJ (2012) Development and validation of the gaming motivation scale (GAMS). Pers Individ Dif 53(7):827–831

Lepper MR, Greene D, Nisbett RE (1973) Undermining children's intrinsic interest with extrinsic reward: a test of the "overjustification" hypothesis. J Pers Soc Psychol 28(1):129–137

Lewis C, Wardrip-Fruin N, Whitehead J (2012) Motivational game design patterns of 'ville games. In: Proceedings of the international conference on the foundations of digital games—FDG '12, ACM, New York, pp 172–179

McEwan M, Johnson D, Wyeth P, Blackler A (2012) Videogame control device impact on the play experience. In: Proceedings of the 8th Australasian conference on interactive entertainment: playing the system (IE '12), ACM, Auckland, New Zealand, pp 1–3

Patall EA, Sylvester BJ, Han C (2014) The role of competence in the effects of choice on motivation. J Exp Soc Psychol 50:27–44

Peng W, Lin JH, Pfeiffer KA, Winn B (2012) Need satisfaction supportive game features as motivational determinants: an experimental study of a self-determination theory guided exergame. Media Psychol 15(2):175–196

Przybylski AK, Weinstein N, Ryan RM, Rigby CS (2009a) Having to versus wanting to play: background and consequences of harmonious versus obsessive engagement in video games. Cyberpsychol Behav 12(5):485–492

Przybylski AK, Ryan RM, Rigby CS (2009b) The motivating role of violence in video games. Pers Soc Psychol Bull 35(2):243–259

Rigby S, Ryan RM (2011) Glued to games. ABC-CLIO, Santa Barbara

Ryan RM, Deci EL (2000a) Intrinsic and extrinsic motivations: classic definitions and new directions. Contemp Educ Psychol 25(1):54–67

Ryan RM, Deci EL (2000b) Self-determination theory and the facilitation of intrinsic motivation, social development, and well-being. Am Psychol 55(1):68–78

Ryan RM, Rigby CS, Przybylski A (2006) The motivational pull of video games: a self-determination theory approach. Motiv Emot 30(4):344–360

Schmierbach M, Chung MY, Wu M, Kim K (2014) No one likes to lose. J Media Psychol 26(3):105–110

Skinner BF (1953) Science and human behavior. Macmillan, New York

Tamborini R, Bowman ND, Eden A, Grizzard M, Organ A (2010) Defining media enjoyment as the satisfaction of intrinsic needs. J Commun 60(4):758–777

Wang CKJ, Khoo A, Liu WC, Divaharan S (2008) Passion and intrinsic motivation in digital gaming. Cyberpsychol Behav 11(1):39–45

Chapter 9
Explorations in Player Motivations: Gamer Profiles

Barbaros Bostan and Guven Catak

Abstract Research on player psychology is gaining increasing attention and this study aims to fill this gap in the literature by empirically exploring the motivational factors of gameplay and defining independent player profiles. Using the psychological need framework defined by Explorations in Personality, 1938, this research collected data from game players ($n = 503$), using a questionnaire. Results of the study found five motivational factors: Affiliation, Power, Achievement, Self-Protection, and Curiosity, and defined six player types: Casual Players, Affiliation Seekers, Power Seekers, Impression Managers, Aggressors, and Intellectuals. This study is unique in that it is capable of recognizing player behavior within a computer game by matching motivational components with individual player actions.

Keywords Computer games • Play • Player psychology • Player profiles • Motives • Needs

9.1 Introduction

Video games are complex, emergent systems of uncertainty, information, and conflict where game players enter into a virtual environment of infinite possibilities, experiencing altered states of consciousness and becoming absorbed in what is happening onscreen (Turkle 1984). The psychological appeal of these virtual experiences that we call video games has been a popular discussion among scholars interested in the cognitive, social, and spatial processes that characterize the concept of "play." Understanding the psychology of the player is also important for

B. Bostan, Ph.D. (✉)
Department of Information Systems and Technologies, Yeditepe University, Istanbul, Turkey
e-mail: bbostan@yeditepe.edu.tr

G. Catak, Ph.D.
Department of Communication Design, Bahcesehir University, Istanbul, Turkey
e-mail: guven.catak@comm.bahcesehir.edu.tr

© Springer International Publishing Switzerland 2016
B. Bostan (ed.), *Gamer Psychology and Behavior*, International Series
on Computer Entertainment and Media Technology,
DOI 10.1007/978-3-319-29904-4_9

game developers and producers (1) to identify the attraction and holding power of games they intend to market for certain audiences (Kallio et al. 2011), (2) to identify the components of player enjoyment/fun and maximize it, (3) to recognize pre-defined player types or behavior within a game and to customize gaming experiences according to the preferences of different groups of players (ongoing research in interactive storytelling systems refer to it as player modeling or player profiling), and (4) to model players in order to instill human-like qualities into non-player characters (Charles and Black 2004). As the scholarly or commercial intention to understand player psychology varies, so does the findings and frameworks defined by scholars and developers.

Two major studies that influenced researchers of player psychology are the intrinsic motivations taxonomy (Malone and Lepper 1987) and the flow framework (Csikszentmihalyi 1990). Although the intrinsic motivations taxonomy was not specifically developed for computer games, it analyzed intrinsic motivations for learning, and defined the individual/interpersonal components of motivation. It cannot be directly applied to gaming; it rather answers the question: "What makes things fun to learn?" The flow framework was applied to computer games by Sweetser and Wyeth (2005) who defined a model for evaluating player enjoyment. Rather than identifying individual player types, the model defines the basics of goal-directed behavior, focusing on both personal and situational factors that influence the motivation to reach a goal. Ten motivations for play in online games have been grouped into three factors by Yee (2006), four gaming motivations (control, context, competency, and engagement) were defined by Kellar et al. (2005), and three motivational factors (autonomy, competence, and relatedness) were defined by Ryan et al. (2006). Discussing the specifics of each variable defined by these studies is beyond the scope of this paper, but Bostan (2009) compared the three major studies in literature (Sweetser and Wyeth 2005; Malone and Lepper 1987; Yee 2006) and found that there is not a single common variable among them.

The four player types of Bartle (2004)—Explorers, Achievers, Socializers, Killers—have also been widely used in literature, but the underlying assumptions of the model have not been empirically tested and the player types have not been shown to be independent and valid. Both Bartle (2004) and Yee (2006) create categories that focus on the structure of current games, rather than looking at fundamental motives and satisfactions that are generic for all games and players (Tychsen et al. 2008). Matching the motivational components and subcomponents defined by Yee (2006) with individual player actions is also still under investigation and some of the hypotheses proposed by researchers are not strongly supported by the data they collect (Suznjevic and Matijasevic 2010). Applying personality measures such as Myers-Briggs typology, Five Factor Model, or trait theories to gaming (Bateman and Boon 2005; Teng 2008, 2009; Zammitto 2010; Park et al. 2011) is also problematic because they fail to explain the majority of game preferences and it is very difficult to match these psychological constructs with individual actions. There are also studies that focus solely on online computer games (Leo Whang and Lee 2004; Tseng 2010; Zackariasson et al. 2010; Hamari and Lehdonvirta 2010; Jansz and Tanis 2007; Williams et al. 2006), mostly Massive Multiplayer Online Role-Playing

Games (MMORPGs), where the generalizability of the results might be questionable. These existing player typologies may be suited to researching or analyzing player psychology in the context of digital games but a diverse range of motivational factors have been proposed across studies with a substantial amount of similarities.

A unified psychology model that takes into account psychological needs, emotional states, moods or feelings, general behavioral patterns, and personality traits would be a major advancement, leading to a whole new set of opportunities for analyzing entertainment experiences and individuals' motivation to use entertainment products for enjoyment. In this regard, Bostan (2009) used a personality model based on the needs framework of Murray (1938), which defines psychological needs by matching them with actions and feelings, appropriate desires and effects, emotions, personality traits, actones (motones and verbones), different forms of need activity (intravertive, subjectified, semi-objectified, egocentric, infravertive, etc.), pathology, social forms and common relationships with other needs such as fusions, conflicts, and subsidizations. Regarding the need framework of Murray (1938), the following questions have already been answered: (1) the study is still applicable since it defines the basic desires and analyzes the multifaceted nature of intrinsic motivation (Reiss 2004), (2) the study is applicable to motivational studies in interactive/new media such as Facebook (Ines and Abdelkader 2011), (3) the study is suitable for gaming, the needs of the framework have already been investigated in relation to various gaming situations that can be experienced in digital role-playing games (RPGs) (Bostan 2009), (4) the framework is capable of identifying the relationship between psychological needs and game mechanics (Bostan and Kaplancali 2009), (5) the framework is capable of analyzing user-created content (mods) of a computer game in terms of the needs they satisfy (Bostan and Kaplancali 2010), (6) the framework can predict goal-directed behavior of both player and non-player characters in a computer game and can be used to design virtual agents with personality (Bostan 2010), and (7) the framework is suitable for customizing the gaming experience in an interactive storytelling system (Bostan and Marsh 2012).

9.2 Purpose of Research

This study attempts to take the above-mentioned studies based on Murray's motivational framework (1938) one step further and to extend the application of the needs framework adaptation to gaming by Bostan (2009). The study aims to answer the following question: Instead of defining a limited number of profiles where the generalizability of the results is questionable, can we use the 27 psychological needs defined by Murray (1938) to define independent player profiles/player types in any game/genre? The first step in answering this question is the selection of multiple games and a single genre to test this hypothesis. The profiles that come out of the statistical analysis will not be generalized because these kinds of player profiles/player types are highly dependent on the selected genre, the selected games, and the game mechanics in each game. Future studies conducted with different genres and different games may come out with different statistical results and thus profiles. But if this need framework is applicable in any genre/game and if it is capable of defining independent player profiles, then we may finally have a reliable framework of motivations for gaming. In terms of motivational studies, RPGs require special attention, since they offer virtual environments analogous to the real world. So, the selected genre for this study is RPGs since they are social and interactive artificial universes with their own rules, politics, culture, ethics, and economy, and thus capable of satisfying the different needs of players.

Although several classifications of needs exist in the literature, this study regards each need as an individual variable of personality and uses the 27 needs and their matching actions defined by the original study (Murray 1938). It is very important to note that questionnaire construction is a delicate activity and the specific wording of each question to be asked is very important. In this study, each question simply lists the actions related with a single need (without naming the need) and respondents were asked to rate the level of importance of the actions in the context of RPGs. The needs investigated are given below and the italic written groups of actions are the questionnaire items themselves:

- Acquisition (nAcq)

  - *To gain possessions and property. To grasp, snatch or steal things. To bargain or gamble. To work for money or goods.*

- Construction (nCons)

  - *To create and build new objects/items. To combine and configure objects.*

- Order (nOrd)

  - *To arrange, organize, put away objects. To be tidy and clean.*

- Retention (nRet)

  - *To retain possession of things. To refuse to give or lend. To hoard. To be frugal, economical and miserly.*

- Aggression (nAgg)

  - *To assault or injure a person. To murder. To belittle, harm, blame, accuse or maliciously ridicule a person.*

- Blamavoidance (nBlam)

  - *To avoid blame or punishment. To be well-behaved and obey the law. To be concerned about public opinion.*

- Counteraction (nCnt)

  - *To overcome defeat by restriving and retaliating. To defend one's honor in action.*

- Defendance (nDfd)

  - *To defend oneself against criticism or blame. To conceal or justify a misdeed, failure or humiliation. To offer extenuations, explanations and excuses.*

- Deference (nDef)

  - *To admire and willingly follow a superior allied person. To co-operate with a leader. To serve gladly.*

- Dominance (nDom)

  - *To influence or control others. To persuade, prohibit, dictate. To lead and direct. To restrain. To organize the behavior of a group.*

- Abasement (nAba)

  - *To surrender. To comply and accept punishment. To apologize, confess, atone. To admit inferiority, error, wrong-doing or defeat.*

- Affiliation (nAff)

  - *To form friendships and associations. To greet, join, and live with others. To co-operate and converse sociably with others. To join groups.*

- Nurturance (nNur)

  - *To nourish, aid or protect a helpless person. To express sympathy. To have a child.*

- Rejection (nRej)

  - *To snub, ignore or exclude a person. To remain aloof and indifferent. To be discriminating. To exclude, abandon, expel, or remain indifferent to an inferior.*

- Succorance (nSuc)

  - *To seek aid, protection or sympathy. To cry for help. To plead for mercy. To be dependent.*

- Achievement (nAch)

  - *To overcome obstacles, to exercise power, to strive to do something difficult as well and as quickly as possible. To excel one's self. To rival and surpass others.*

- Autonomy (nAuto)

  - *To resist influence or coercion. To defy an authority or seek freedom. To strive for independence.*

- Harmavoidance (nHarm)

  - *To avoid pain, physical injury, illness and death. To escape from a dangerous situation. To take precautionary measures.*

- Infavoidance (nInf)

  - *To avoid failure, shame, humiliation, ridicule. To refrain from attempting to do something that is beyond one's powers. To conceal a disfigurement.*

- Recognition (nRec)

  - *To excite praise and commendation. To demand respect. To boast and exhibit one's accomplishments. To seek distinction, social prestige, honours or high office.*

- Exhibition (nExh)

  - *To attract attention to one's person. To excite, amuse, stir, shock, thrill others. To make an impression. To be seen and heard.*

- Cognizance (nCog)

  - *To ask questions. To satisfy curiosity. To look, listen, inspect. To read and seek knowledge.*

- Exposition (nExp)

  - *To point and demonstrate. To relate facts. To give information, explain, interpret, lecture.*

- Understanding (nUnd)

  - *To analyze experience; to abstract; to discriminate among concepts; to define relations; to synthesize ideas and arrive at generalizations*

- Play (nPlay)

  - *To relax, amuse oneself, seek diversion and entertainment. To 'have fun,' to laugh, joke and be merry.*

- Sentience (nSen)

  - *To seek and enjoy sensuous impressions such as pleasurable sights (color, light, form, movement, a beautiful face, clothes, decoration, landscapes, architecture, painting and sculpture) and pleasurable sounds (natural sounds, human voice, poetry and music).*

- Sex (nSex)

  - *To form and further an erotic relationship. To have sexual intercourse.*

9.3 Methodology and Results

Twenty-seven questions were generated and each question consists of a number of actions associated with a single need by Murray (1938). Players used a 5-point response format, where 1=unimportant, 2=of little importance, 3=moderately important, 4=important, and 5=very important. Respondents were asked to rate the level of importance of the actions listed in each question in the context of RPGs. The action groupings were based on Murray's 3-year study at the Harvard Psychological Clinic, which was conducted by 28 psychologists of various schools, among whom were three physicians and five psychoanalysts. After the questionnaire was prepared, data were collected from 503 RPG players through online surveys publicized at online portals that catered to RPG players from several popular RPGs—*Elder Scrolls V: Skyrim*, *The Witcher 2* and *Kingdoms of Amalur: Reckoning*. In the context of game studies, if researchers have not experienced the game personally, they are liable to commit severe misunderstandings, even if they study the mechanics and try their best to guess at their workings (Aarseth 2003). As an obligation to understand gameplay, all the selected games have been finished by the author(s) several times.

9.3.1 Descriptive Statistics

Table 9.1 shows that the gamers displayed moderately high scores in Cognizance, Play, Achievement, Sentience, and Counteraction. They reported low scores in Succorance, Rejection, Sex, Abasement, and Aggression. Thus, to explore, to seek diversion and entertainment, to overcome obstacles, to seek and enjoy sensuous impressions such as pleasurable sights and pleasurable sounds, to restrive and retaliate, and to finish challenging tasks are the most important actions for players. The lowest scores implicate that players are not interested in seeking aid, protection or sympathy, to snub, ignore, or exclude a person, to form and further an erotic relationship, and to surrender. Another noteworthy statistics is that aggression has a relatively lower mean than most of the variables. The negative effects of gaming and violence in video games have been a popular debate among researchers but players are not inclined toward aggressive, combative, or destructive behavior. However, a remarkable portion of the playtime is spent with killing other people/creatures since the game mechanics impose the players to do so. Frequency table for aggression, which is related with the following actions: to assault or injure a person, to murder, to belittle, harm, blame, or accuse, is given below (Table 9.2).

Table 9.1 Descriptive statistics of key variables

	Mean	SD		Mean	SD		Mean	SD
nAba	2.15	1.114	nExp	3	1.099	nDef	2.71	1.085
nAch	4.13	0.954	nHarm	3.47	1.189	nDfd	2.41	1.143
nAcq	3.72	0.945	nInf	2.49	1.141	nDom	3.13	1.168
nAff	3.48	1.184	nNur	3.34	1.149	nExh	2.88	1.158
nAgg	2.28	1.198	nOrd	3.23	1.155	nSen	4.11	0.979
nAuto	3.68	1.112	nPlay	4.16	0.978	nSex	2.07	1.174
nBlam	2.57	1.102	nRec	3.06	1.175	nSuc	1.85	0.943
nCnt	3.86	0.97	nRej	1.86	1.009	nUnd	3.52	1.035
nCog	4.27	0.858	nRet	2.65	1.14	nCons	3.57	1.046

Table 9.2 Frequency table for aggression

nAgg

		Frequency	Percent	Valid percent	Cumulative percent
Valid	1	159	31.6	31.6	31.6
	2	165	32.8	32.8	64.4
	3	90	17.9	17.9	82.3
	4	58	11.5	11.5	93.8
	5	31	6.2	6.2	100
	Total	503	100	100	

9.3.2 Factor Analytic Insights

A principal component analysis (PCA) was conducted on the 27 items with orthogonal rotation (varimax). A sample of size 503 is considered quite satisfactory for this research since Comrey and Lee (1992) and Tabachnick and Fidell (2007) defined a sample size of 300 as satisfactory. Kass and Tinsley (1979) recommended having between 5 and 10 participants per variable up to a total of 300. The Kaiser–Meyer–Olkin measure verified the sampling adequacy for the analysis, KMO = 0.786 — "good" according to Field (2009). Bartlett's test of sphericity $\chi^2(351) =$ 2913.59, $p < 0.001$, indicated that correlations between items were sufficiently large for PCA and the factor model is appropriate. An initial analysis was run to obtain eigenvalues for each component in the data. Eight components had eigenvalues over Kaiser's criterion of 1 and in combination explained 56.42 % of the variance. The factor with an eigenvalue of 1.019 is not retained in the analysis since it is barely above 1. Finally, seven components were extracted and in combination they explained 52.64 % of the variance (Table 9.3).

After the components were extracted, reliability analysis was run on each one of them. Although a value of 0.7–0.8 is an acceptable value for Cronbach's alpha, when dealing with psychological constructs, values below even 0.7 can realistically be expected because of the diversity of the constructs being measured (Kline 1999). Subscale 1 appears to have good internal consistency with $\alpha = 0.785$. The removal of Harmavoidance increases the α value of Subscale 4 to 0.639 and the removal of Play increases the α value of Subscale 2 to 0.599. Thus, Subscales 2 and 4 have α values close to 0.7. Subscales 3 and 6 have α values above 0.50 and thus relatively lower reliability but they are retained in the study until the cluster analysis. Since Subscales 5 and 7 have α values below 0.40, they are removed from the analysis. Table 9.4 shows the final subscales and the corresponding Cronbach's α values.

9.3.3 Cluster Analysis of Variables

Cluster analysis determines how many "natural" groups there are in the sample and the aim is to (1) minimize variability within clusters and (2) maximize variability between clusters. Complete linkage, between-groups linkage and within-groups

Table 9.3 Factor analysis subscales

1	2	3	4	5	6	7
Succorance	Aggression	Recognition	Infavoidance	Sentience	Understanding	Acquisition
Abasement	Rejection	Exhibition	Defendance	Autonomy	Exposition	Retention
Deference	Dominance	Achievement	Blameavoidance	Sex	Cognizance	Construction
Affiliation	Play	Counteraction	Harmavoidance			Order
Nurturance						

Table 9.4 Final factor analysis subscales

1	2	3	4	5
$\alpha=0.785$	$\alpha=0.599$	$\alpha=0.655$	$\alpha=0.639$	$\alpha=0.558$
Succorance	Aggression	Recognition	Infavoidance	Understanding
Abasement	Rejection	Exhibition	Defendance	Exposition
Deference	Dominance	Achievement	Blameavoidance	Cognizance
Affiliation		Counteraction		
Nurturance				

Table 9.5 Cluster analysis of variables

Between-groups linkage cluster membership		Within-groups linkage cluster membership		Complete linkage cluster membership	
Case	5 Clusters	Case	5 Clusters	Case	5 Clusters
nDom	1	nDom	1	nDom	1
nAgg	1	nAgg	1	nAgg	1
nRej	1	nRej	1	nRej	1
nAch	2	nAch	2	nAch	2
nRec	2	nRec	2	nRec	2
nExh	2	nExh	2	nExh	2
nCnt	2	nCnt	2	nCnt	2
nInf	3	nInf	3	nInf	3
nDfd	3	nDfd	3	nDfd	3
nAff	4	nBlam	3	nAff	4
nAba	4	nAff	4	nAba	4
nNur	4	nAba	4	nNur	4
nSuc	4	nNur	4	nSuc	4
nDef	4	nSuc	4	nDef	4
nBlam	4	nDef	4	nBlam	4
nCog	5	nExp	4	nCog	5
nUnd	5	nCog	5	nUnd	5
nExp	5	nUnd	5	nExp	5

linkage hierarchical cluster analyses with Pearson correlations as a distance measure was used to examine the structure of the remaining 18 variables. Since five factors were retained from the factor analysis, the number of clusters is specified as five. When the cluster membership tables were consulted, it is seen that the factor structure from the factor analysis is replicated with 94 % accuracy in the clusters. The only exceptions are: blameavoidance in between-groups and complete linkage methods and Exhibition in within-groups linkage method. With an exception of one variable in each method, 17 of the 18 variables form clusters identical to the factor structure as shown in Table 9.5.

Since the cluster analysis of variables confirms the subscales of the factor analysis, five remaining factors are retained in the study. The first one, which consists of Succorance, Abasement, Deference, Affiliation, and Nurturance, is named as Affiliation. The second one, which consists of Aggression, Rejection, and Dominance, is named as Power. The third one, which consists of Recognition, Exhibition, Achievement, and Counteraction, is named as Achievement. The fourth one, which consists of Infavoidance, Defendance, Blameavoidance, and Harmavoidance, is named as Self-Protection. The final one, which consists of Understanding, Exposition, and Cognition, is named as Curiosity. Among the five factors, affiliation, power, and achievement are three major motivations in literature (Heckhausen and Heckhausen 1988). Self-protection is an instance of self-evaluation motive that represents the desire to maximize the positivity and minimize the negativity (Sedikides and Alicke 2012). Curiosity is an old concept in the study of human motivation and it is a source of inquiring, learning, and exploring (Silvia 2012). Curiosity motivates people to fill gaps of knowledge, to explore, and to learn. The five factors are calculated as follows:

1. Affiliation: $nSuc + nAba + nDef + nAff + nNur$
2. Power: $nAgg + nRej + nDom$
3. Achievement: $nRec + nExh + nAch + nCnt$
4. Self-Protection: $nInf + nDfd + nBlam$
5. Curiosity: $nUnd + nExp + nCog$

9.3.4 Cluster Analysis of Cases

Cluster analysis was used to look for "subpopulations" of gamers with respect to the remaining 18 reliable motivational variables. The cluster method chosen was the within-groups linkage and the dissimilarity measure chosen was the "pearson correlation." Table 9.6 displays the last 10 fusions of the agglomeration schedule, that is, the agglomeration coefficients for the respective number of clusters. The agglomeration coefficients showed a rather larger increase from 2 to 3, 5 to 6, and 8 to 9 clusters. Since 3 clusters might be too few and 9 clusters might be too much for interpretation, we decided to terminate at the 497th fusion stage. The six-cluster solution also produces meaningful relationships with the five factors of this study when an ANOVA is conducted.

Among the 6 gamer clusters, 3 represent 71.3 % and 4 represent 86.6 % of the total population. Clusters 1, 5, 3, and 2 are the dominant subpopulations, whereas clusters 4 and 6 are minorities. Table 9.7 shows the frequency and percentage of each gamer cluster. After the cluster analysis of 503 cases, it is important to identify the contribution of each (affiliation, power, achievement, self-protection, and curiosity) factor to each gamer cluster. To identify these relationships, the clustering variable CLU6_1 is used for further analysis.

Table 9.6 Agglomeration schedule of the cluster analysis of cases

Number of clusters	Agglomeration coefficient	Differences in coefficient	Percent change in coefficient
10	0.767	0.002	0.222
9	0.765	0.011	1.478
8	0.754	0.003	0.372
7	0.751	0.000	0.064
6	0.751	0.008	1.070
5	0.743	0.004	0.527
4	0.739	0.001	0.122
3	0.738	0.014	2.001
2	0.724	0.012	1.744
1	0.711		

Table 9.7 Gamer cluster frequencies

Average Linkage (within group)

		Frequency	Percent	Valid percent	Cumulative percent
Clusters	1	126	25	25	25
	2	77	15.3	15.3	40.4
	3	105	20.9	20.9	61.2
	4	34	6.8	6.8	68
	5	128	25.4	25.4	93.4
	6	33	6.6	6.6	100
	Total	503	100	100	

9.3.5 Findings of ANOVA

Prior to the ANOVA, Levene's test for equality of variances was performed, and all the tests were not significant (Factor 1: $p=0.842$; Factor 2: $p=0.066$; Factor 3: $p=0.242$; Factor 4: $p=0.171$; Factor 5: $p=0.129$). Thus, the variances in the manipulation groups are not different and therefore the assumptions for ANOVA are met. Since factor analysis was used to find orthogonal factors that make up the dependent variables, univariate ANOVAs on each factor should be unrelated. ANOVA results in the Table 9.8 indicate that the Factor 1 ($F(5497)=17,214$, $p<0.001$), Factor 2 ($F(5497)=21,537$, $p<0.001$), Factor 3 ($F(5497)=50,699$, $p<0.001$), Factor 4 ($F(5497)=3105$, $p<0.01$), and Factor 5 ($F(5497)=17,575$, $p<0.001$) are significantly correlated with the clustering variable CLU6_1.

9.4 Discussion

The study identified six clusters of gamers related with five factors derived from psychological needs. Cluster 1, which has the highest mean in Affiliation, lowest mean in Power, low mean in Achievement, highest mean in Self-protection, and

Table 9.8 ANOVA

ANOVA		Sum of squares	df	Mean square	F	Sig.
Factor 1	Between groups	1084.848	5	216.970	17.214	0.000
	Within groups	6264.146	497	12.604		
	Total	7348.994	502			
Factor 2	Between groups	568.218	5	113.644	21.537	0.000
	Within groups	2622.550	497	5277		
	Total	3190.767	502			
Factor 3	Between groups	1524.494	5	304.899	50.699	0.000
	Within groups	2988.929	497	6014		
	Total	4513.423	502			
Factor 4	Between groups	101.261	5	20.252	3105	0.009
	Within groups	3241.880	497	6523		
	Total	3343.141	502			
Factor 5	Between groups	361.947	5	72.389	17.575	0.000
	Within groups	2047.134	497	4119		
	Total	2409.082	502			

Table 9.9 Frequencies of player types

Casual players (%)	Affiliation seekers (%)	Power seekers (%)	Impression managers (%)	Aggressors (%)	Intellectuals (%)
25.4	25	20.9	15.3	6.8	6.6

average mean in Curiosity is named Affiliation Seekers. Cluster 2, which has an average mean in Affiliation, low mean in Power, highest mean in Achievement, high mean in Self-protection, and lowest mean in Curiosity is named Impression Managers. Cluster 3, which has a low mean in Affiliation, high mean in Power, average mean in Achievement, low mean in Self-protection and high mean in Curiosity, is named Power Seekers. Cluster 4, which has the lowest mean in Affiliation, highest mean in Power, high mean in Achievement, lowest mean in Self-protection, and low mean in Curiosity, is named Aggressors. Cluster 5, which has an average value in all five factors, is named Casual Players. Cluster 6, which has a high mean in Affiliation, average mean in Power, lowest mean in Achievement, average mean in Self-protection, and highest mean in Curiosity is named Intellectuals. Table 9.9 shows the frequencies of the player types defined above. The findings are also visualized in Fig. 9.1.

Affiliation seekers are interested in forming new relationships but needs such as recognition, exhibition, achievement, aggression, and domination are not a priority for them. They value knowledge and since most game mechanics force them to fight/challenge opponents, they prize self-protection so that they will be able to survive these encounters. Individuals high in affiliation motivation tend to initiate fewer acts that might spark conflict and specific affiliation-related goals include: being in the company of others, cooperating, exchanging information, and being

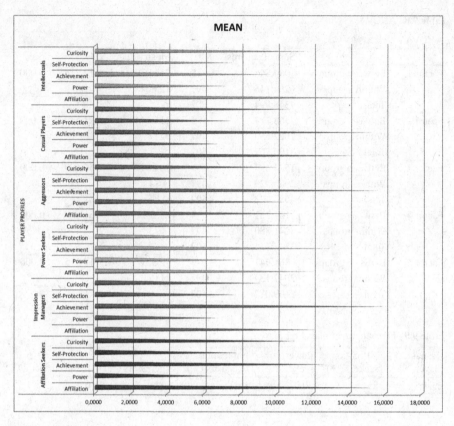

Fig. 9.1 Player profiles

friends (Merrick et al. 2011). *Impression managers* are not interested in knowledge and power, but they are motivated for affiliation and self-protection. The driving motivation for these players is achievement; they are natural achievers interested in recognition, exhibition, and counteraction. These players resemble the self-validator players of Heeter et al. (2009) who seek prestige and like to win but dislike losing so they would prefer an easy victory to a challenge where the probability of failing is high. *Power seekers* do not value relationships and self-protection but they do believe that curiosity/knowledge is power. They are interested in having a reputation and they are aggressive players who dominate others for power. These players are competitive and goal-oriented, they win at all costs. *Aggressors* are distinctively identified by having the lowest values in affiliation and self-protection. They are not playing the game for social relationships and they do compensate their lack of self-protection by their aggressiveness. Since they do have the highest value for power, it can be argued that they are also power seekers but high aggression and low harm avoidance is a distinctive feature for killers. *Casual players* who have average values in all the motivational factors are players who do not focus on a single motivation.

They are understood to be a more diverse group who play for fun or to kill time, have little knowledge about game conventions, and play few games (Sotamaa 2007). These players are similar to Wanderers defined by Bateman and Boon (2005) who are less challenge-oriented than other players and who seek new, constant, undemanding, and fun experiences. *Intellectuals* are not playing the game for reputation or power but they do value social relationships and knowledge above all. Intellectuals are motivated by intrinsic factors such as curiosity, role play, and learning.

It should be noted that player profiling requires constant monitoring of the player actions within the virtual world. Player actions shall give an idea about his/her preferences or needs, but it should not be forgotten that the restrictions imposed by the game mechanics significantly reduce the number of player needs satisfied by a game. For instance, if a quest requires the player to kill an opponent when he/she has no other option, then the act of killing cannot be considered as an inclination toward aggressive behavior. It can be considered so only when the player has other options. For example, in popular PRG titles, the player usually notices the enemies before the enemies notice the player, and it is up to the player how he/she overcomes obstacles. Some alternatives are to ignore the enemy by sneaking from a safe distance (Harmavoidance), to directly attack the enemy with a weapon of choice (Aggression), or to sneak to a favorable position and eliminate the enemy quickly taking advantage of surprise and without receiving much damage in the process (Aggression and Harmavoidance fusion). It is these choices in a computer game that determine the play style of a player and indicate his/her trends in motivation. But the player's actions before the choice are also important determinants for understanding his/her motivations of the player. If the player is low in health and ammunition before the choice, it is understandable why he/she avoids a powerful group of monsters (Harmavoidance inhibiting Aggression). Moreover, the actions after the enemy is eliminated are also indicators of player intent. One who loots every single enemy after the combat (Acquisition) is not like the one who ignores the dead bodies and proceeds to his/her next quest destination (Achievement). And even the one who loots and retains possession of every single item (Retention) is satisfying different needs than the one who only loots ammo/weapons (Aggression). These complex motivational interactions require constant monitoring of player actions and these actions should be suitable for matching them with the motivational variables used for player profiling. Motivation-action mappings is the critical key for psychological player profiles.

This study claims that the motivational framework adaptation to gaming by Bostan (2009) (1) can define empirically tested, independent, and valid player profiles; (2) can function outside of the narrow context of Bartle's player stereotypes; (3) can differentiate the underlying basic categories of motivations between player profiles; (4) can explain player profiles without statistical shortcomings; and (5) can match motivational components with individual player actions. Since the questionnaire was promoted on online gaming forums, there is a possibility of sampling bias, as those who frequent these online forums may represent the most enthusiastic and dedicated members of a gaming community (McMahon et al. 2012).

Future research will be conducted in a variety of game genres to validate the usability of motivational variables in player profiling but we do not aim to generalize the six clusters of gamers defined by this study. Since the motivation-action mappings can be applied to any computer game, our claim is that the motivational framework used in this study is applicable to any genre.

References

Aarseth E (2003) Playing research: methodological approaches to game analysis. In Proceedings of the 5th international digital arts and culture conference (MelbourneDAC)

Bartle RA (2004) Designing virtual worlds. New Riders Publishing, Indianapolis

Bateman C, Boon R (2005) 21st century game design. Charles River Media, London

Bostan B (2009) Player motivations: a psychological perspective. ACM Comput Entertain 7(2). http://dl.acm.org/citation.cfm?doid=1541895.1541902

Bostan B (2010) A motivational framework for analyzing player and virtual agent behavior. Entertain Comput 1(3–4):139–146. doi:10.1016/j.entcom.2010.09.002

Bostan B, Kaplancali U (2009) Explorations in player motivations: game mechanics. In Proceedings of GAMEON 2009, Düsseldorf, Germany

Bostan B, Kaplancali U (2010) Explorations in player motivations: game mods. In Proceedings of GAMEON-ASIA 2010, Shanghai, China

Bostan B, Marsh T (2012) Fundamentals of interactive storytelling. Acad J Inform Technol 3(8):19–42, www.ajit-e.org/download_pdf.php?id=46&f=46_rev1.pdf

Charles D, Black M (2004) Dynamic player modeling: a framework for player-centered digital games. In Proceedings of the international conference on computer games: artificial intelligence, design and education, pp 29–35

Comrey AL, Lee HB (1992) A first course in factor analysis. Erlbaum, Hillsdale

Csikszentmihalyi M (1990) Flow: the psychology of optimal experience. Harper Perennial, New York

Field AP (2009) Discovering statistics using SPSS. Sage Publications, London

Hamari J, Lehdonvirta V (2010) Game design as marketing: how game mechanics create demand for virtual goods. Int J Bus Sci Appl Manage 5(1):14–29

Heckhausen J, Heckhausen H (1988) Motivation and action, Munich

Heeter C, Magerko B, Medler B, Fitzgerald J (2009) Game design and the challenge-avoiding self-validator player type. Int J Games Comput-Mediated Simul 1(3):53–67

Ines DL, Abdelkader G (2011) Facebook games: between social and personal aspects. Int J Comput Inform Syst Indust Manage Appl 3:713–723

Jansz J, Tanis M (2007) Appeal of playing online first person shooter games. Cyberpsychol Behav 10(1):133–136

Kallio KP, Mäyrä F, Kaipainen K (2011) At least nine ways to play: approaching gamer mentalities. Games Cult 6(4):327–353

Kass RA, Tinsley HEA (1979) Factor analysis. J Leis Res 11:120–138

Kellar M, Watters C, Duffy J (2005) Motivational factors in game play in two user groups. In Proceedings of the DIGRA 2007 Conference (Tokyo, Japan), pp 1–8

Kline P (1999) The handbook of psychological testing. Routledge, London

Leo Whang SM, Lee SJ (2004) Lifestyles of virtual world residents: living in the on-line game "lineage". Cyberpsychol Behav 7(5):592–600

Malone TW, Lepper MR (1987) Making learning fun: a taxonomy of intrinsic motivations for learning. In: Snow RE, Farr MJ (eds) Aptitude, learning, and instruction: conative and affective process analyses. Lawrence Erlbaum, Hillsdale

McMahon N, Wyeth P, Johnson D (2012) Personality and player types in Fallout New Vegas. In Proceedings of the 4th international conference on fun and games, Association for Computing Machinery, Toulouse, pp 113–116

Merrick K, Gu N, Niazi M, Shafi K (2011) Motivation, cyberworlds and collective design. In Circuit bending, breaking and mending: proceedings of the 16th international conference on computer-aided architectural design research in Asia, pp 697–706

Murray HA (1938) Explorations in personality. Oxford University Press, New York

Park J, Song Y, Teng C-I (2011) Exploring the links between personality traits and motivations to play online games. Cyberpsychol Behav Soc Netw 14(12):747–751. doi:10.1089/cyber. 2010.0502

Reiss S (2004) Multifaceted nature of intrinsic motivation: the theory of 16 basic desires. Rev Gen Psychol 8(3):179–193

Ryan RM, Rigby CS, Przybylski A (2006) The motivational pull of video games: a self determination theory approach. Motiv Emot 30(4):347–364

Sedikides C, Alicke MD (2012) Self-enhancement and self-protection motives. In: Ryan RM (ed) Oxford handbook of motivation. Oxford University Press, New York, pp 303–322

Silvia PJ (2012) Curiosity and motivation. In: Ryan RM (ed) The Oxford handbook of human motivation. Oxford University Press, New York, pp 157–166

Sotamaa O (2007) Perceptions of player in game design literature. Situated play: proceedings of the 2007 digital games research association conference, pp 456–465

Suznjevic M, Matijasevic M (2010) Why MMORPG players do what they do: relating motivations to action categories. Int J Adv Media Commun 4(4):405–424

Sweetser P, Wyeth P (2005) GameFlow: a model for evaluating player enjoyment in games. ACM Comput Entertain 3(3). http://dl.acm.org/citation.cfm?doid=1077246.1077253

Tabachnick GG, Fidell LS (2007) Experimental designs using ANOVA. Duxbury, Belmont

Teng C-I (2008) Personality differences between online game players and non-players in a student sample. Cyberpsychol Behav 11(2):232–234

Teng C-I (2009) Online game player personality and real-life need fulfillment. Int J Cyber Soc Educ 2(2):39–50

Tseng F-C (2010) Segmenting online gamers by motivation. Expert Syst Appl 38:7693–7697

Turkle S (1984) The second self: computers and the human spirit. Simon & Schuster, New York

Tychsen A, Hitchens M, Brolund T (2008) Motivations for play in computer role-playing games. Proceedings of future play 2008, Toronto, Canada, pp 57–64

Williams D, Ducheneaut N, Xiong L, Zhang Y, Yee N, Nickell E (2006) From tree house to barracks: the social life of guilds in World of Warcraft. Games Cult 1(4):338–361

Yee N (2006) Motivations of play in online games. Cyberpsychol Behav 9(6):772–775

Zackariasson P, Wåhlin N, Wilson TL (2010) Virtual identities and market segmentation in marketing in and through massively multiplayer online games (MMOGs). Serv Mark Q 31:275–295

Zammitto VL (2010) Gamers' personality and their gaming preferences. Master Thesis, School of Interactive Arts and Technology, University of Belgrano

Printed in the United States
By Bookmasters